EDUCATION
FOR
LEISURE

EDUCATION
FOR
LEISURE

H. DAN CORBIN

WILLIAM J. TAIT

PRENTICE-HALL, INC.
Englewood Cliffs, New Jersey

LIBRARY OF CONGRESS CATALOGING IN PUBLICATION DATA

CORBIN, H DAN.
  Education for leisure.

  Bibliography: p.
  1. Leisure. 2. Recreation. I. Tait, William J.,
joint author. II. Title.
BJ1498.C66   790'.07   72–10840
ISBN 0–13–240531–8

*To the late Jay B. Nash,
whose pioneer efforts as a leader,
administrator, teacher, and philosopher
have left an indelible mark on a field
dedicated to optimum development
and enrichment of the individual.*

Printed in the United States of America

10   9   8   7   6   5   4   3   2   1

*Prentice-Hall International, Inc.,*London
*Prentice-Hall of Australia, Pty. Ltd.,*Sydney
*Prentice-Hall of Canada, Ltd.,*Toronto
Prentice-Hall of India Private Limited,
New Delhi
*Prentice-Hall of Japan, Inc.,*Tokyo

CONTENTS

chapter three

BASIC HUMAN DEVELOPMENTAL PATTERNS　　31

chapter four

THE ROLE OF LEISURE-RECREATION
IN SATISFYING MAN'S NEEDS　　49

chapter five

THE SCHOOL AND EDUCATION FOR LEISURE　　59

chapter six

PUBLIC RECREATION　　77

PREFACE

The goal of this book is the worthy use of leisure. Every level of education should contribute toward this end, especially recreation education.

Expanding leisure time and increasing affluence subject the uninitiated and poorly prepared individual to overwhelming pressures, often opposed to his best interests. The need for genuine concern for individual dignity and worth, reflected in leisure-time pursuits, is greater now than at any time in our nation's history. It calls for communitywide efforts to improve the quality of leisure activities. These developments make it more necessary than ever to involve the various levels of the public school systems and higher education in the acquisition of leisure skill and appreciation. We have dedicated our efforts to achieving an intensive and concerted attempt to improve education for leisure.

We most appreciatively acknowledge the indelible contributions of the pioneers of the recreation movement, particularly Jay B. Nash, under whose influence we fell in graduate school. Because of our association with Dr. Nash, our philosophies markedly resemble his.

In addition, we thank our secretaries, Mrs. Shirley Mitchell and Mrs. Sandra Gifford, for their invaluable and extremely patient help.

H. Dan Corbin is Professor and Chairman of the Recreation Education Section, Purdue University. William J. Tait is Professor Emeritus and former Chairman of the Recreation Curriculum at Florida State University.

"ARE YOU *SURE* THIS IS THE *ACTUAL START*
OF HIS 'EDUCATION FOR LEISURE'?"

chapter one

LEISURE - BLESSING
OR BLIGHT?

*Education today has before it many new
jobs. It is doubtful, though, whether any of
them is greater than the job of educating
for freedom in its most literal form. The
bounty consists not only of more leisure
hours but of increased life expectancy. If all
that were required was increased emphasis
on hobbies, the problem would be
nonexistent. What is actually required is the
making of a new man—someone who has
confidence in the limitless possibilities of his
own development, someone who is not
intimidated by the prospect of an open
hour, someone who is aware that science
may be able to make an easier world but
only man can make a better one.*

NORMAN COUSINS

CHANGING VALUES

If you had twenty dollars in your pocket and no classes or work
to go to, what would you do? Our value systems determine the leisure
activities in which we participate, and our choice of leisure activities
shapes the cultural patterns of our community. Value systems change
slowly. Recent protests, demonstrations, and riots indicate that people's
values are changing at the present time. During the past one hundred
years we valued industrial growth and production most highly. The
industrial era was preceded by an agricultural era, in which farm production was the dominant influence on people's value systems. Today
the poverty, welfare, and rehabilitation programs and the drive toward
minority group rights indicate the ever-increasing demand for, and
high value placed on, human services.

3

CHANGING CONCEPT OF LEISURE

For centuries our ancestors have believed that man's salvation lies in his work. Sayings such as "Play is the work of children" and "Idle hands are the devil's workshop" constantly reinforced work as the most important value. Today, with technology furnishing the necessities of life in greater abundance, we place the quality of life ahead of industrial production. We have more time to devote to the pursuit of happiness.

INCREASE OF LEISURE

Leisure used to be the reward for work. The Christian ethic was "Six days shall ye work and on the seventh day shall ye rest." Today the work week is five days long, and we are seriously experimenting with a four-day work week. Technical advances have decreased work schedules, increasing our leisure time. Automation has changed our life style. Our twenty-four-hour day consists of eight hours of sleep, two hours devoted to eating and personal care, eight hours of work, and six hours of leisure; on weekends, most people schedule no work.

> *Check your time schedule. Keep a daily diary for a week, accounting for fifteen-minute units of time. How many hours of leisure do you have?*

In analyzing your week, note that some of your activities are consistently routine. The fact of living involves sleep, meals, and personal care (such as bathing, toilet, and grooming), over which you exercise little choice. Periodically, you may shift your sleeping or eating schedules to accommodate an unusual situation (to cram for an exam, for example), but you actually have little choice over whether you eat or sleep.

OBLIGATED TIME

Sociologists point out that we have *obligated* and *unobligated* time. If you join an organization (church, fraternity, sorority, club), you obligate yourself to spend some time pursuing that activity. Some people obligate most of their time and lead a highly organized life. They are always hurrying to a meeting, cannot sit still, complain that there are too few hours in the day, and feel guilty if they take a coffee break.

UNOBLIGATED TIME

Unobligated time is often referred to as free time. Free time is the small units of time between scheduled activities. Sometimes we can, by tight scheduling, collect these units into a sizable parcel; however, we may then be apt to schedule that collected parcel, and the free time becomes obligated time.

LEISURE TIME

For too long we have associated leisure with time. Leisure is an attitude toward life; it reflects our value system as we select activities for our pattern of living. If you ask an American what he does, he immediately tells you his vocation: I am an engineer, an accountant, a salesman. Ask a European the same question and he replies, I am a hiker, a violinist, a painter, a collector of butterflies. The answers reflect the different value systems of the two cultures.

WORK ETHIC–LEISURE ETHIC

It seems logical that we should adjust our value system to upgrade the quality of life, particularly with the increasing amount of time available for leisure. The work ethic as the center of living is giving way to the leisure ethic. Recently the work ethic has been questioned as a result of the technical advances of automation. Not only can machines produce a greater volume of products in less time, but the nature of the job (work) has also changed. Many positions requiring craftsmen's skills (wheelwright, typist) have been replaced by machines. The person has been removed one or more units from the product. For example, the wheelwright watches a wheel-stamping machine punch out a former week's work in minutes; the typist hooks the dictating machine to a typewriter to produce a letter. The personal pride of production is removed and people lose the satisfaction of contributing directly to society. Another job shift is toward specialization and organization, which narrow the challenge and lead to early boredom on the job. For instance, butchers, who formerly spent much of their time selling to customers, now stand in the back room away from the customers, cutting, pricing, and packaging meat that is then displayed for customer selection. Not all jobs are so unrewarding, but the majority are simple routines and the number of jobs so affected is increasing rapidly. The advertising slogan "Machines work, people think" has validity and an impact on our way of life.

> *How many people are involved in menial work? Look up labor statistics and compare the number of workers in each job classification. What percent of workers are professional? blue collar? white collar? managers? clerical? sales? craftsmen? Can man find recreation in his work? Discuss.*

IMPORTANCE OF LEISURE

The importance of leisure in our personal lives cannot be overestimated. Let us summarize the main reasons for its importance.

Psychological (mental) health. Only leisure can rehabilitate the overstressed mechanism of the mind. Stress in today's world has many sources. The frustrations of poverty, unemployment, overwork, or incompatibility with surroundings affect a large part of our population. Mere idleness is not the answer. The kind of leisure men need in a machine-age civilization is a spare-time interest that uses their intelligence and restores their self-respect.

Physical health. Man is biologically a creature designed for active participation. You must use your muscles to keep them functioning. Lifetime sports programs and physical activities have dominated our recreation offerings so much that many people think of physical activity as the only form of recreation.

Avenue for self-expression. One of man's basic needs is to communicate—to be recognized for his contribution to society. Because of our automated society we have lost opportunities to design and create products that reflect the worker. No longer do glass blowers, cobblers, wheelwrights, and other artisans personally produce their products. Leisure, with its variety of activities, is man's main outlet for individual self-expression.

Continual development. Man is not a stagnant creature. He is continually developing and changing. We can and do become locked into situations where life grows very routine and unchallenging and does not allow change. In such circumstances leisure programs provide a challenge to learn something new and encourage people to develop. Pursuing a hobby often leads to adopting that hobby as a vocation. Leisure allows for experimentation.

Big business. Everyone is directly concerned economically with leisure. People spend between 15 and 25 percent of their income directly on leisure-recreation. The problem of deciding what expenditures should be classified as leisure-recreation accounts for the percentage difference. For example, does gasoline for the car count as transportation to work or as joy-riding? Is the cost of eating out accountable to leisure or part of the food budget? The number of people employed by leisure-centered industries and services has grown. The December 28, 1959 issue of *Life Magazine* was entirely devoted to the economics of leisure: "forty billion dollar bill just for fun."

Basic needs. Most of our opportunities for meeting the following needs are in leisure:

Recognition—people seek your opinion and company
Status—you are the president of the club, play first violin, or are the coach
Self-direction—you make the decisions directly
Group acceptance—people want and depend upon your presence
New experiences—you try sky-diving, gourmet cooking, camping
Self-expression—you speak out at a forum, paint a picture, create a dance

LEISURE-RECREATION

We tend to use the words *leisure* and *recreation* interchangeably. In the past, recreation has been popularly connected with physical activity. Many still cling to that point of view even though they recognize that recreational activities can and do encompass a large variety of nonphysical pursuits, such as reading, art, music, drama, and discussions.

> *Compare attendance at sports events, museums, the performing arts; compare expenditures for sports equipment, art supplies, books, travel.[1] Do the comparisons reflect people's values?*

PSYCHOLOGICAL VALUE

The wide range of leisure activity has both a psychological and a physical effect on us, and encourages the use of the term *leisure* instead of *recreation*. We accept the gestalt psychology of the "whole" man, which says that experiences that affect the physical being also affect the psychological being. Man cannot be segmented. This does not mean that all people enter into an activity consciously to help the

---

[1] *Statistical Abstract of the United States.* Use the latest edition; it is published annually by the Bureau of the Census, United States Department of Commerce, United States Government Printing Office.

"whole self." Most of our participation is motivated by a single major purpose; the many other values of the activity are incidental or subconscious. For instance, on a hot summer day I decide to go swimming. I recognize that I am hot and uncomfortable, but it does not occur to me to take a cold shower. My friends are at the pool, so I socialize for two hours, swim for ten minutes, sun on the dock for fifty minutes, return home refreshed, and tell everyone I had to cool off—and I believe myself. The situation could be reversed; I could go for socialization and companionship and return refreshed in body because of the exercise involved in swimming.

PLANNED ACTIVITY

Do people plan their leisure activities, or do the activities occur spontaneously? Many people feel that recreation and leisure must be unplanned, spontaneous fun during "free time." Although their idea sounds attractive, it does not fit into many of our lives. Most people follow a daily routine, scheduling their activities to get the most out of life. The work ethic pushes us to reject anything that is not purposeful or that is wasteful, lazy, or inefficient. It has eliminated some free time from our lives as we attempt to increase efficiency. The "happy hour" aboard ship, the "coffee break" at the office, and the "koffee klatch" in the neighborhood are examples of organized free time.

We obligate much of our time by joining organizations and setting up routines. People feel uncomfortable without a basic routine to follow. Very few live unscheduled lives. One of the greatest deterrents to retirement is the fear of not having anything to do. "How would I use all that time?" is a real problem to people who now follow a fairly rigid routine.

Another problem is the opposite reaction, boredom. When people have accepted and performed routine tasks, the challenge of innovation diminishes. The prescribed task becomes automatic, fewer decisions are required, and they grow bored. When a textile company automated its plant and hired ten mechanics to maintain the machines, the manager had to insist that the mechanics keep away from the machines and fix only those machines that had actually stopped. The number of breakdowns decreased 30 percent when mechanics were not allowed to observe machines in action and "make adjustments."

How routine is your life? How long do you go to school or church or play ball before you wish you had a few days off? How long do you enjoy a vacation when there is no plan or schedule of activity? When was the last time you had "nothing to do?"

PATTERNS OF LIVING

Leisure living is great for those who are self-motivated and continually seek new things to do. It is fearful to those who feel trapped or insecure. When people become bored with their drab routine, what do they do during their leisure?

What interests or hobbies do you pursue during your leisure? Has your interest changed in the last year? List what you think are the most popular activities? Are they the same for each age group?

Studies of living patterns have been made periodically.[2] The Athletic Institute each year publishes a list of the ten top participant sports in rank order.[3]

List the ten sports you think would have the greatest participation. Then check your list against the list prepared by the Athletic Institute for this year.

If you are a lover of art you will appreciate the fact that the Metropolitan Museum of Modern Art is visited daily by four times the number of people accommodated at Madison Square Garden for a basketball game. As you critically examine some of these statistical facts, you can make some comparisons that will surprise you (remember that you have been greatly influenced by gossip, television, radio, newspapers, magazines, and so on).

Try to find at least five other surprising statistics on how we spend our money in leisure-time pursuits.

CENTERS FOR THE STUDY OF LEISURE

We have been slow to accept the idea of leisure for all people and to study its effect on our lives. In 1955 the Center for the Study of

[2] An excellent historical source with a good bibliography is Eric Larrabee and Ralph Meyersohn, *Mass Leisure* (New York: The Free Press, 1958).

[3] Athletic Institute, "The Leading Participant Sports." Write to Athletic Institute, Merchandise Mart Building, Chicago, Illinois 60654.

Leisure was established at the University of Chicago, funded by a grant from the Ford Foundation. Dr. David Riesman, the noted sociologist, was made chairman of the center, which had five professional staff members. The Center's purpose was to give direction to and intensify the studies of leisure and mass communications which were underway in several departments in the University. A policy of diversity of approach within three outstanding areas was followed. These areas were research in the suburbs, research in the industrial setting, and research in the mass media. Some miscellaneous activities were conducted, including a study of mass phenomena, such as fads, as one important process in leisure habits; a statistical analysis of the role of education in recreation expenditures; a study of American travel from 1900 to 1950; and a bibliography of books and articles. The Center was discontinued in 1960 as the personnel shifted to other institutions.

The Institute for Studies of Leisure was begun in 1969 at the University of South Florida in Tampa. Dr. Max Kaplan heads the Institute, which is responsible to the University's Center for Research and Development. Because the Institute is both regional and national in scope, it has both community and international advisory boards. The Institute began in response to the need in the United States for a major center to deal boldly and systematically with issues of leisure. Among these are the human impact of cybernation, economic and political transformations (such as the guaranteed annual wage), a philosophy for abundant time and increasing affluence, classlessness in consuming patterns, the extension of significant nonwork commitments, expanding adult education, principles for counseling in the use of new time-bulks, preparation for retirement, and so on. No other center existed in the United States to deal with these issues under government, university, or private auspices.

The Institute program was planned to develop research publications, conferences, a special library, educational films, and demonstration programs. It was also designed to work with an Institute on Aging, also begun in 1969 at the University of South Florida. The Institute has held several international conferences on leisure, publishes a newsletter, and conducts studies.

Other countries have been much more interested in leisure than the United States. At present eighteen countries have some form of special center or institute for the study of leisure: Belgium, Canada, Czechoslovakia, Denmark, Finland, France, East Germany, West Germany, Great Britain, Hungary, Italy, the Netherlands, Norway, Poland, Sweden, Switzerland, the U.S.S.R., and Yugoslavia. All these centers cooperate, with UNESCO as a coordinating agency. The European Center for Leisure and Education was located in Prague, Czechoslovakia in 1968 and publishes reports in English. Probably the best-known leader in the field of leisure is Professor Jaffre Dumazadier of France, whose book *Toward a Society of Leisure* (translated from the French by Stewart E. McClure) is fascinating reading.

SUMMARY

In this brief overview, you have met the concept that leisure, like other facets of life, is in a state of flux. Whether the change results in leisure's being a blessing or a blight on society will depend on how well we can educate for leisure.

Selected Reading

BRIGHTBILL, CHARLES K., *The Challenge of Leisure.* Englewood Cliffs, N.J.: Prentice-Hall, 1963.

DE GRAZIA, SEBASTIAN, *Of Time, Work and Leisure.* New York: Doubleday, 1964.

DUMAZADIER, JOFFRE, *Toward a Society of Leisure,* trans. Stewart McClure. New York: The Free Press, 1967.

GOODE, WILLIAM J., ed., *Readings on the Family and Society.* Englewood Cliffs, N.J.: Prentice-Hall, 1964.

HOFFER, ERIC, *The Ordeal of Change.* New York: Harper & Row, 1963.

KAPLAN, MAX, *Leisure in America. A Social Inquiry.* New York: John Wiley, 1960.

KLEEMEIER, ROBERT W., *Aging and Leisure.* New York: Oxford University Press, 1961.

LARRABEE, ERIC, and ROLF MEYERSOHN, eds., *Mass Leisure.* New York: The Free Press, 1958.

MEYER, HAROLD; CHARLES BRIGHTBILL, and H. DOUGLAS SESSOMS, *Community Recreation: A Guide to Its Organization* (4th ed.). Englewood Cliffs, N.J.: Prentice-Hall, 1969.

NASH, JAY B., *Recreation: Pertinent Readings.* Dubuque, Iowa: W C Brown, 1964.

PROSHANSKY, HAROLD, WILLIAM I. HELSON, and LANUE RIVLIN, eds., *Environmental Psychology: Man and His Physical Setting.* New York: Holt, Rinehart and Winston, 1970.

WATTENBERG, BEN J., *This U.S.A.* New York: Doubleday & Company, Inc., 1965.

"ONE THING THAT SEEMS TO BE GETTING POPULAR IS CALLED 'WORK'."

chapter two

LEISURE-
AGENT
FOR CHANGE

*For there still remains the biggest problem
of modern man—perhaps even bigger than
war: what to do with himself. As he ceases
to be a creature of endless toil, poverty, and
famine, he is apt to find himself liberated
into nothingness. His leisure time can
become more of a curse than the plagues of
old.*

NORMAN COUSINS

Nothing is so constant as change.
We live in an era of rapid social change: the new math befuddles
parents who try to help with Junior's homework, priests are marrying,
universities have coed dormitories.

THEORIES CHANGE

The changes that have occurred during man's history appear to
have been very gradual. If we examine major changes in life style, it
becomes apparent that the most rapid rate of change accompanies
man's gaining control of some form of energy. When man learned to
control and even to produce fire, he became nomadic—a great change
in life style. When he invented wheels and levers, he was able to move
and control materials and to build the pyramids and cities. When man
learned to control electricity and steam, the Industrial Revolution

changed his agrarian life to an urban one. His latest achievement, the control of atomic energy, should forewarn us of a coming rapid change in our present living pattern.

"Change or die," some ecologists tell us. They say that man has gone too far in his quest for material production and that he must change his exploiting attitude toward nature, before it is too late.

Have you changed? What is change? Your reply to these questions depends largely on your age and on the length of time you are considering. A common belief is that change has taken place only if violent and/or drastic rearrangements have recently occurred in a person's life. Change is not always recognized in the gradual shifts in attitudes, values, economic levels, acquisition of material luxury items, and so on.

There are two major points of view regarding change. One is that mankind never changes. The past repeats itself. According to this cyclic, historical point of view, mankind repeats the same actions he has taken in the past. Man has remained essentially the same for the past two thousand years.

The second and opposite point of view is that change is constant. Change improves man's life, and it can be recognized. Man should and does change in adapting to different environmental living conditions.

PHYSICAL CHANGE

Few people recognize change in themselves or in those they see daily. Do you recognize any changes in your parents or immediate members of your family? Have you recently visited close friends of four or five years ago and been amazed at how much they have changed? This is particularly true in older age groups, where drastic changes occur in a person's appearance at certain stages of life. Physical alterations vividly portray change, for example, gaining a great deal of weight, becoming bald, growing long hair, or assuming a beard. We often fail to recognize even old friends. It is difficult to evaluate change in individuals you see on a frequent or daily basis, but easy to tell the changes in people you see only occasionally. If you think there has been little change in your ideas, attitudes, or physical appearance over the past year, perhaps you should ask yourself whether you are *living* or just *existing*—because to live is to be constantly changing.

What effect does it have on your friends when you assume a new hairdo or a wig, grow a mustache, change the style of your eyeglasses, or buy a "mod" outfit? We often change our ways but hesitate to communicate the change to others. We try to project the image of what we would like our friends to think we are, even though we have changed. Hypocritical role playing is a fault of which youth accuses the older generation. Reflect the true you; your employer may require you to project a certain image at work, but during your leisure, your real values should show.

ATTITUDE CHANGE

Man needs self-confidence. His decision-making processes depend upon his value judgments, and a person who does not have the confidence of his convictions leads a very insecure life, often reflected in extremes of behavior. If you have not changed, consider this question: Are you willing to examine your values and points of view? Do you think that you are always right? Have you made up your mind on topics, and would you rather not be confused with the facts? Too often people refuse to give up the security of their convictions. Change threatens that security, even if change would be for the better. In our growth toward urbanization, we are having to make more and more decisions which no longer concern only ourselves, but can also affect the lives of many other people.[1]

Whether or not you have changed, you should consider many factors while forming opinions of our society. Let us briefly review the changes that have occurred in your lifetime in the United States and the world. To gain insight into personal values, talk to your older brother or sister and see what he or she remembers. Your mother and father will re-

[1] Four excellent studies of our changing world are Don Fabun, *The Dynamics of Change* (Englewood Cliffs, N.J.: Prentice-Hall, 1970), reprinted from the six issues of the *Kaiser Aluminum News* devoted to changes in America; Alvin Toffler, *Future Shock* (New York: Random House, 1970); Eric Hoffer; *The Temper of Our Time* (New York: Harper & Row, Publishers, 1967); and Arnold Toynbee; *Change and Habit: The Challenge of Our Time* (New York: Oxford University Press, 1966). To illustrate the population explosion, Fabun relates that from 1946, the world's population has increased by about 2 percent each year. In six hundred fifty years—less time than from the Renaissance to the present—there will be one person standing on each square foot of land, if the present growth rate continues.

member another era and other events that shaped their values. They will emphasize specific events and issues to try to arrange your value systems in accordance with their own. Your grandmother or grandfather's anecdotes of the past will reveal how life was lived then. They tend to emphasize the "good old days," which is normal because we often forget some of our adverse times, preferring to remember the better times.

> *Examine the changes that have occurred within the last five years of your life. Then go back ten or even twenty years and see what you can remember.*

After the twenty-year mark you probably must depend on written history and on stories that have been passed down. Scenes recorded in movies, on sound tapes, and by other means of communication remind you of past situations. The scenes that stand out will not be the ordinary items, but those which involved a great deal of stress and emotion. As we look back, we will perhaps recount the wars and the economic problems that faced our country periodically. We tend to lose track of time and dates, but we remember outstanding events that had a marked influence on people.

> *Talk to your neighbors and list some of the events that were factors in changing their lives.*

CHANGE IN OUR WORLD

Few of us, from the very young to the very old, are without opinion when it comes to interpreting past events and their importance. However, our opinions differ immensely, depending again on our age, our values, and our knowledge of the subject. An expert historian would have a completely different view of life during the Gay Nineties than would your great-grandmother. World War II is probably not nearly as important to some as the invention of television. Most of us interpret events according to how they affect our daily lives, rather than how they affect society as a whole.

What is your opinion of (1) the first manned rockets or a flight into space, (2) the development of the Salk vaccine to stamp out infantile paralysis, (3) the dropping of the atomic bomb, (4) the Depression of the 1930s, (5) World War I, (6) the Gay 1890s? When was the Continental Rail System linked by the golden spike? Were there electric lights one hundred years ago?

The farther back we go, the fewer events we remember and the more nebulous is our relationship with the past. We recognize the physical changes that have occurred, but they seem to have much less meaning to us personally. To discover the psychological influences on men's value systems, we should perhaps review the Black Panther movement, the Nazi rise in Germany, the Victorian Era in England, serfdom, absolute monarchies, the Ming dynasty in China, the Mayan culture of the South American Incas, the stone age tribes of Mindanao in the Philippines, and even cave men and the discovery of fire and the wheel. But the farther we delve into the past, the less we connect it with the present and the less we discern its effect on our lives today.

Looking at the past, however, helps us develop a frame of reference for studying critically modern living patterns and for recognizing that change is continually happening. Few school children today have any conception of the technical developments that have affected their lives. Most of us assume that we can go to a store and buy any food at any time; we would not have been so lucky a few decades ago. Our grandparents had to wait until summer to enjoy lettuce, tomatoes, and other truck-farm products that could only be eaten in season. However, today we can even throw snowballs in the middle of July, and the refrigeration that allows us to do so is taken for granted.

Now let us turn from the past to some concepts that will have a great effect upon the future of our country, concepts that are developing slowly but should be accelerated to improve man's life.

CHANGING CONCEPTS OF TIME

You will recognize that not all concepts of time are widely accepted. Examine them to determine which will lead us to richer lives and a better society.

The Work Day

One time concept that has changed is the rigidity of the eight-hour day, the forty-hour week, and the fifty-week year. While the small independent businessman and some professional people in service-oriented occupations still spend more time on the job, electricians and other blue-collar technicians are working a thirty-two hour week and even, in some cases, a twenty-four hour week.

Is it necessary that we work from 8 AM to 5 PM? The workday, traditionally geared to daylight hours, has seen many changes. New ideas have led to widespread acceptance of the summertime daylight savings plan. We move our clocks ahead one hour so that we can take advantage of more sunlight hours for recreation and/or leisure. Some employees are now negotiating with their bosses to be paid for the product they make and not for the amount of time spent in producing it. Many self-employed people could choose any working hours between 10 in the morning and 2 the next morning. There is no valid or logical reason why we cannot adjust the required working time and allow more flexibility. Companies and groups of workers can shift their time and work loads so that production is not disturbed. In fact, such a shift may increase production, as people work when they prefer to and at their own pace. Some companies are trying and accepting changes in working hours because of snarled traffic patterns. In large cities traffic is at a peak at 8 AM and again at 5 PM; to avoid traffic jams, many companies have staggered their office hours.

When you consider the flexibility of time and people's changing concepts of its use, you can see that many changes could be effected. Experts have suggested that the crime rate would decrease if more people were abroad in the neighborhoods at all times during the day and night. Empty streets promote a feeling of aloneness; no one seems to be concerned about others' actions. It is intriguing to imagine how the various problems of mass transit and of water and electrical supply would vanish if we could shift people's time schedules and spread use of these products more evenly over a twenty-four-hour period.

The Work Week

In the past people worked six or seven days a week. Today the five-day week is accepted. It is possible that an even shorter work week could be implemented—a three-day week, for example. We would have long weekends with free time or at least a choice of what to do. Such choices involve leisure or discretionary time. Different people choose different leisure activities; many obligate much of their time by joining organized groups and establishing a full schedule of activity, while others prefer not to obligate their time but to determine their activities daily. Between the extremes, most people try to balance their daily routines with some obligated activity and some free time. The more the individual determines how he spends his hours, the better his living conditions.

Vacations

Another changing concept of time concerns vacations. Most work agreements today call for accrual of vacation time at a rate of one day per month of service, accumulating to two weeks or, in many cases, up to a month's paid vacation per year. Many companies are accepting an escalation clause based on longevity: the longer you work for a company, the more vacation time you receive. A five-year veteran employee may receive a month's vacation, a ten-year employee two months, and so on. Vacation schedules should be examined closely, and vacation time used to better advantage. Instead of taking a vacation every August, as usual, many people now vacation at varied times of the year. Some take shorter vacations more often; for example, if a worker has two weeks of vacation, he may take one in January and another in July. Scattering vacations throughout the year to achieve a periodic change in routine has merit. It could possibly increase production and, simultaneously, increase the value of living.

Year-round Schools

There has been much talk about twelve-month school schedules. It is no longer necessary for children to attend school during the winter months so that they can have the summer free to help with the harvest. Year-round production schedules and urban living conditions have changed all that. Air conditioning makes it unnecessary to leave our hot cities in the summer. But if the children are out of school then family vacations must be taken when the children are available. Many couples without children are able to take their vacations at any time.

Taking several vacations a year, none of them long enough to be a major disruption of a work routine, has advantages. Many companies encourage employees to take vacations throughout the year or to accumulate vacation time for a particular activity. If you want to travel to Europe, you accumulate a two-month vacation by "banking" your vacation time. Such flexible arrangements are appealing to employees and worth the extra time required for arrangements. After an extended trip, you can work longer or harder than usual to make up the production that you missed during the vacation.

Most of our ideas concerning time, work, and leisure are throwbacks to an age when work was considered sacred and leisure practically sinful. The Puritan Ethic of working for work's sake no longer applies to our highly technical age, in which machines do much of the work. Many of our attitudes need to be redesigned and reevaluated.

> *If you, rather than your employer, determined how you spend your time, what would you do? List the activities you would choose, making a daily time schedule for the next two weeks.*

CHANGING PATTERNS OF LIVING

Our patterns of living reflect our value systems, although there are discrepancies between our life styles and the reasons we give to justify our values. This "cultural lag" is a source of discontent. One section of society says, "Tell it like it is" or "Show what you really do, not what you tell me you *want* to do."

Value Systems

Our value systems dictate our routines (we arise at 7 AM because we have to get to work at 8 AM). We place a high value on production and try to increase the gross national product. Our pattern of living becomes subservient to the production line.

The following questions and comments about the total structure of organization in the business world were raised at a top-level conference of economics and business leaders in Denver, Colorado in 1967.

Can we develop a system that would allow workers more flexibility in determining their time on the job? For instance, could a worker put in two twelve-hour days in succession and be off for the next five days? Perhaps one worker would choose to work three months, including weekends, to accumulate vacation time for a long trip. The reality of banking hours of time, much as we now accumulate and bank money, will probably come in the near future.

Can we have a guaranteed annual wage? Some workers are now demanding a guaranteed volume of work.

The traditional emphasis of labor on work conditions and rate of pay has shifted to fringe benefits and full employment.

What are industry's responsibilities in regard to personnel benefits in the areas of retirement, vacations, and insurance?

What will happen to the worker when the average work week drops below twenty hours and approaches five to ten hours? Is the work ethic so strong that he will "moonlight" two positions? Are there enough jobs for the population?

If we placed a higher value on people than on products, our pattern of living would change. Many modern young people are "people-centered," as we can readily see in articles which express concern about overpopulation, ecology, our environment, and our interpretation of the laws to protect individual rights in our society. These changes in basic concepts change our patterns of living. Man strives to conform with society, yet seeks to maintain his individuality.

Our attitudes are affected by our patterns of living. For example, the young adult (twenty-five to thirty years of age) is not concerned about saving money for emergencies and for old age if hospital insurance and retirement pension are automatically deducted from his paycheck. We have built into our community living many systems that leave no decisions to the individual. This was not always true, and it is probably most evident in young people's attitudes toward money, as contrasted with those of their parents, particularly if the parents were children during the Depression years of 1930–40.

Rural to Urban Shift

One of the main shifts in our pattern of living has been the change from a rural to an urban society. Fifty years ago three-fourths of our people lived on the land, leading a rural, isolated life. Now three-fourths of our population lead an urban existence characterized by increasing population density. Urbanization has created social problems that have been described by David Riesman in *The Lonely Crowd*.[2] Accompanying urbanization has been a sense of isolationism that allows people to do what they want without regard for their neighbors. In almost every urban community people in the same apartment building are strangers! Increased technology has intensified our isolation. In the past we sat on the back porch to cool off during the summer, and there we would converse with our neighbors, who were on their porches. Today we stay in air conditioned rooms in hot weather and in heated rooms in cold weather. Affluence has provided most families with all the necessities and many of the luxuries of living. We no longer borrow things from our neighbors; we would rather rent them. Our independence results in social isolation.

Housing

We are becoming a nation of apartment dwellers. Sixty percent of all new building permits are for multi-family units, compared to 30 percent in 1960. The increase in the number of apartment complexes is much greater than that of individual housing, partly because of a slowly changing economic system. The money lenders, a conservative element of our society, hesitate to loan money on new, unproven ideas (mobile homes, modular homes, new materials and designs). The interest rate on a loan for a small, traditional single-family dwelling is often beyond the individual's reach; money is available at a lower rate for building large housing complexes.

Mobility

Another change in the pattern of living is the mobility of large segments of our population. We can be anywhere in the United States within four to six hours. Commuting fifty miles from home to work every day is no longer a problem. We tend to change jobs and/or homes with great facility. The length of time during which the individual is associated with a particular group has become shorter. Mobility tends to increase our independence, with its accompanying isolation.

[2]David Riesman et al., *The Lonely Crowd: A Study of the Changing American Character* (rev. ed.) (New Haven, Conn.: Yale University Press, 1950).

Employment

Employment opportunities may also change. The volume of production may increase while job opportunities become scarcer with the automation of factories. The computer has all but replaced many clerical workers, and the development of more sophisticated machinery to do man's work leads to technical change.

> *What changes do you anticipate in your living pattern within the next two years?*

TECHNOLOGICAL CHANGE

To discuss all the technical changes that have occurred in the last few years would take many volumes. Possibly the most dramatic technical change is man's ability to conquer outer space, but the world of electronics and aerospace is only part of the many changes that affect our lives. We are increasing our knowledge so rapidly that it doubles every ten years. Some people say, "Don't confuse me with more information. I already know I'm not doing what I should be doing!"

Mass Communication

An example is the advance of mass communications technology. We used to depend upon newspapers for our information. Our literacy rate was fairly high, but today, with radio and television, we have access to more information and immediate coverage. If an accident occurs on the corner, the people in the next town know about it as soon as the people down the street. We can watch the death and destruction caused by earthquakes, war, floods, and other catastrophes—live and in color—on our television sets. The death of the man down the street affects us less and less as we become accustomed to watching great calamities the world over. We are becoming immune to our fellow man's suffering because of overexposure to it.

Machinery

Another big technical change is the improvement of machinery. Modern automobiles, for example, have sophisticated power brakes, steering wheels, stereos, radio, television, computerized fuel injection, and so on. The modern housewife who complains that she needs a maid really needs a mechanic to keep all her household appliances working. She needs technical help with the vacuum cleaner, the air conditioner, the automatic stove, and the myriad other gadgets we have developed and incorporated into our living patterns. Cybernetics and the development of "black boxes" to replace people have done away with many tedious tasks. Not all the changes brought by the computer improve our life, however; an example is the frequent errors in computerized bills.

Transportation

A technical change that has affected our social attitudes is the availability of mass transportation. One can visit anyplace in the country at any time. This easy accessibility of distant places may potentially increase understanding among the nation's subcultures. Northerners can get a firsthand look at the rural South and thereby better understand its problems. Conversely, a Texan from the wide open spaces can see and better understand the people- and factory-jammed urban areas of the Northeast. However, while improved transportation has the potential to increase understanding, it has yet to accomplish its potential. People still live in the ghettoes without going beyond a five-block radius from their tenement homes. They have not experienced mobility and the understanding that comes with it.

SOCIOLOGICAL CHANGES IN THE UNITED STATES

Socially, people change very slowly. New ideas do not gain wide acceptance in short periods of time. However, mass communication and greater mobility have contributed greatly to sociological change in America, by bringing social differences to the foreground. Communication and mobility have increased the rate of change in our social relations, our ideas, and our value systems. Real and disturbing social issues presently confront our society. The most important problem is probably race relations and the treatment of minority groups in the United

States. Change for the better has been tremendous and continues. Universal acceptance of all people, however, is far in the future.

Job Status

Another change in social concepts and values concerns job status. In the future we will still find vestiges of the traditional classifications: professional, white-collar, blue-collar, and laborer. However, even now many people judge others by their personal qualities and the contribution they make to society. Leisure activities involving groups of people with a common interest contribute to the breakdown of economically-based classes. The city symphony orchestra may include a clerk, a judge, and a plumber practicing together and sharing their love of classical music.

Education

Parallel to job status is educational status. We have put great value on continuing education. As society matures, there is greater acceptance of new ideas and of the individual's right to change his position. Education provides an opportunity to change vocations, if the individual desires to do so, creating greater job mobility and thus greater social mobility.

Religion

One of the most dramatic developments is the change in our attitudes toward traditional Christian mores. More and more people are questioning the older ways of doing things. Changes include the folk mass church service, the variety of nontraditional marriage ceremonies designed by young people, the frank discussions among people seeking satisfying answers to social problems (abortion, drugs, war), the discarding of particular styles of dress by religious sects, the recognition of holidays of non-Christian origin, the ban of prayer in public schools.

You cannot pick up a newspaper, listen to a television or radio broadcast, or read a magazine without confronting many of the social issues of today. Many people are concerned about your way of life and are trying to influence it, through advertising and the mass communications media. Few individuals escape the continual bombardment of ideas and requests to change their way of life by investing in the latest products.

Social Class

We are becoming a relatively classless society, or at least a one-class society. One of the factors that contributes to this classlessness is the availability of luxury physical goods that are now considered necessities. Very few people live without television, radio, a refrigerator, a car. The aristocrat on the right side of the tracks may have a twenty-four inch color television in a fine mahogany case, but the slum family is listening to the same programs, even though on a less fancy set.

Possibly the biggest factor of sociological change is the polarization of our population on social issues. Recently this has been particularly evident, as groups demand action and take conflicting positions. People are much better informed today than ten years ago. They are bombarded with communications that enable them to make judgments which they are willing to express to others. These factors tend to polarize people at either end of issues.

Legal Change

The more we practice a particular pattern of living, the more we tend to accept it as the correct one for us, and the less flexible we become. When a majority of people in a community accept a particular living pattern, it becomes reflected by regulations and laws in their legal structure. Inheritors of this legal structure may have difficulty amending or repealing laws. Legislating living patterns creates a less flexible, more rigid society with less room for individualism. For example, the number of so-called "blue laws" still on the books, forbidding business or pleasure on Sundays, is astounding.

> *Obtain a copy of your local city code. Mark all the laws or regulations you were unaware of which affect your living pattern.*

PHYSIOLOGICAL CHANGES

Size

Open your newspaper to the sports page and you will find, particularly in the spring, accounts of our seven-foot basketball players. This is a dramatic example of how our size, height, and weight have changed. Most historical museums have displays of knights' armor, which would fit a modern ten-year-old. If you could inspect King Tut's tomb in Egypt, you would find that most of our ancestors were of very small stature.

Health

Our changing physical appearance has meant a change in ways of living in terms of food distribution, consumption, and nutrition. We know a lot about nutrition and its effect on building the body. The college athlete's diet is carefully controlled to put on or take off weight. Two-hundred-and-fifty-pound tackles don't just happen, they are grown. Most of us eat three meals a day; some skip breakfast and eat lunch, dinner, and between-meal snacks. Consuming various nutritional foods in balanced proportion has a direct effect on our life expectancy, contributing to a happier life with less disease and fewer infirmities. People's life expectancy has increased considerably and seems still to be increasing. In 1920, the average life expectancy was 56.3 years; in 1970 it was 69.3. Over ten thousand people in the United States have reached their one hundredth birthday.

What is your life expectancy?

Your insurance rate, your age of retirement, and your social security payments are all based upon life expectancy. We have made great strides toward finding cures for many of the so-called "incurable" diseases. Now that we can control disease, people's size and weight, and to some extent their behavioral characteristics, we should be able to affect our way of living.

SUMMARY

We have briefly tried to explain how our changing world has developed. The heritage of the past has affected much of your present way of life. Examine your values; are they based on fact or fantasy? On superstition or good information? Are they logical? Your life will be happier and more fulfilling if you recognize why you believe as you do.

We have suggested some of the problems we face today. Tomorrow there will be different problems to which you will have to adjust. If you can find a logical and factual reason for a change, it seems imperative that you accept the change as being for the best. Living in the past slows down the process of social change. You can speed up change and live more effectively tomorrow if you look ahead and anticipate changes.

Changes occur during man's leisure time. You control your leisure; when you have a leisure moment, you decide what to do. You may experiment to find a sounder pattern of living, a change in procedure. The more you accept a particular pattern of living, the more you tend to think that you have found the answer, and the less flexible and open to experimentation you become. If you legislate habitual patterns of life, you create a rigid society with little individualism. What do we prize most, individualism or community development? The answer is in the social guides (laws, customs, traditions, mores) concerning our use of leisure.

Everyone searches for a balanced life. To achieve balance, you must answer some basic questions: What is more important—my individuality or my community? My security or my self-realization and self-growth? Should I change, or do I really like my life as it is? Our answers to these questions today, and even more so in the future, will depend on society's approach and attitude toward leisure. As man has more and more free time, he will have to make more and more personal decisions. Society's attitude toward leisure and toward the use of leisure will profoundly affect the quality of our life.

Suggested Reading

BAIER, KURT, and NICHOLAS RESCHER, eds., *Values and the Future*. New York: The Free Press, 1969.

BELL, DANIEL, *Toward the Year Two Thousand*. Boston: Beacon Press, 1969.

FABUN, DON, *The Dynamics of Change*. Englewood Cliffs, N.J.: Prentice-Hall, 1967.

GREER, SCOTT A., *The Emerging City*. New York: The Free Press, 1962.

HOFFER, ERIC, *The Temper of Our Time*. New York: Harper & Row, Publishers, 1967.

HUXLEY, ALDOUS, *Brave New World Revisited*. New York: Harper & Row, 1958.

HUXLEY, JULIAN, *New Bottles for New Wine*. New York: Harper & Row, 1957.

PRIESTLEY, J. B., *Man and Time*. New York: Dell, 1968.

SCHON, DONALD A., *Technology and Change. New York: Dell, 1967.*

SHELDON, ELEANOR B., and WILBERT E. MOORE, *Indicators of Social Change: Concepts and Measurements.* New York: Russell Sage Foundation, 1968.

TOFFLER, ALVIN, *Future Shock.* New York: Random House, 1970.

chapter three

BASIC
HUMAN
DEVELOPMENTAL
PATTERNS

*We should be able not only to work well
but to use leisure well, for the first principle
of all action is leisure. Both are required,
but leisure is better than work and is its end.*

ARISTOTLE

The more we study man, the more we realize how complex an organism he is. For many years we have considered man an individual, created singly just as snowflakes are created singly. His fingerprints are unique and many of his developmental patterns—his personal traits—reinforce our belief that all men are individuals and therefore must be treated as such.

We strive to recognize individuality, but at the same time, to contact many people, we do some homogeneous grouping for leisure activities. Man's developmental pattern is fairly well-defined. As we try to group people together, we realize that people do not develop at the same rate. Grouping by age in leisure activity is not as accurate as grouping by other characteristics, such as physical traits, social compatibility, skill, dexterity, or maturity.

Our application of human developmental patterns to leisure has been assumed more than enunciated, and very little has been written about the effect of leisure on the maturing process in man. We have studied extensively the developmental aspects of childhood. For example, we have detailed almost to the hour and minute what happens from the fertilization of the egg to the emergence of the newborn infant. Such detailed information is helpful to technicians such as doctors who face problems that must be surmounted if the fetus is to become a normal human being.

AGE CLASSIFICATION

It is just as important to know details of man's development throughout the rest of his life span, which in America is now approximately seventy years. Teachers study in great detail the developmental pattern of students between the ages of six and eighteen, with more emphasis on development patterns of the earlier (elementary) years and little if any on development during the later (high school) years. High school teachers tend to be hired because of their subject matter knowledge rather than because of any human development knowledge. This is a fault of our society. We tend to disregard adults as individuals. We assume that they can be on their own and we give them very little personal guidance after the age of eighteen or twenty-one. In reality, people continue to develop throughout their lives and face as many acute problems at age fifty or fifty-five as at age six, nine, one, or three.

Many studies of basic human developmental patterns have been made; yet the details of such research are conflicting. Here we can only summarize some of the major points of view and ask you as a student to look into the other materials that have been developed. As you read these few summary pages, try to remember your own development and identify your place in the continuum as suggested by various scholars.

Some developmental psychologists have suggested the following age classification:

0–10	Formative years
10–20	Frenetic-flippant-fluid-future years
20–30	Foundation years
30–40	Family years
40–60	Middle years
60–up	Terminal years

Disraeli is reputed to have said that youth is a blunder, manhood a struggle, and old age a regret. A Greek proverb ruled that childhood ends at twelve, youth at eighteen, love at twenty, faith at thirty, hope at forty, and desire at fifty. Another generally accepted age classification is as follows:

0–2	Infancy
2–5	Preschool
5–12	Childhood
12–17	Adolescence
17–25	Early maturity
25–50	Maturity
50–75	Late maturity
75–up	Old age

Another perhaps more complete classification system divides the life cycle into sixteen stages:

Conception	Zygote stage
Up to seven weeks	Embryo stage
After seven weeks	Fetus stage
38 Weeks	Birth
Up to 18 months	Infancy
Up to 5 years	Preschool
Up to 11–13 years	Elementary
11–16 years	Puberty and senior high school
15–21 years	Late adolescence
21–25 years	Early adulthood
25–40 years	Middle adulthood
49–60 years	Late adulthood
60–65 years	Preretirement
65–70 years	Retirement
70–years and up	Old age
Terminal illness and death	Senescense

All these classification schemes have one thing in common: they observe that man's development slows down the older he gets. For example, the preschool age group encompasses only three years, while maturity encompasses twenty-five years. Even so, changes occur in adults more frequently than the classification systems indicate. One scholar has suggested two-year groupings for younger people and five-year groupings for those over twenty-five. Whenever we group people we find that some mature earlier and faster than the majority, others later and slower. Adjusting our age groupings to the majority means that groups must overlap.

TRANSITIONS

A movement from one stage of development to another is often accompanied by or coexistent with a definite event in the life of the individual. Consider the advent of a baby's first tooth, or the day he first walks by himself—what a change takes place in that individual at that particular stage of development! Some further examples of events that signify change follow.

The first day in school
The first bicycle
Changing schools, or graduation from elementary to middle school to high school
The advent of puberty, evidenced by physical changes such as the first menstrual flow, breast development, deepening voice, growth of facial hair
The first date
The first driver's license, first permission to use the family car alone
The first job and paycheck
The first legal drink
Marriage
The first child

Many of these events are involved in the leisure activities of the individual. It is obvious that the effect that leisure activities can have upon individual development is of tremendous significance.

To this point we have primarily considered classification systems based on age groups. Erik Erikson's book *Childhood and Society*[1] describes eight stages of man, defining maturity as the successful resolution of the eight stages of ego development (regardless of the age at which maturity is achieved). Each stage is expressed in polar extremes, the first listed being the more desirable trait. Progress during life is seen

[1]Erik Erikson, *Childhood and Society* (rev. ed.) (New York: W. W. Norton & Company, Inc., 1964).

along a continuum from one stage to the next, even though individuals mature at different rates. The eight stages follow:

1. *"Trust versus distrust"* (early infancy). This stage may be exemplified by the first social achievement of the infant: letting its mother out of sight without anxiety or rage. The infant has formed a positive "trust." Its mother has become an inner-certainty to it; it is predictable that she will return.

2. *"Autonomy versus doubt and shame"* (later infancy). If denied gradual and well-guided experience of the autonomy of free choice, the child will doubt his own judgment. He will overmanipulate himself and develop a precocious conscience. A child wants to do things himself and be successful. Imagine the problem a mother creates if she punishes, scorns, or shames her baby's first attempts at feeding himself because he is messy and unskilled. Her constant remonstrances make him doubt his decisions and actions.

3. *"Initiative versus guilt"* (early childhood). The child's wish for autonomy makes him concentrate on excluding potential rivals; therefore, often expresses jealous rage against encroachments such as a younger brother's or sister's demands for their mother's attention. Initiative is accompanied by anticipatory rivalry. For example, a child playing along in his back yard invites a neighbor to enter and offers him the chance to play with a toy. His act of sharing is learned behavior and is a step toward initiative.

The child who first attempts to enter the domain of another child who is bigger, more skilled, and more established will generally meet with rebuff and little success. Constant rebuffs could direct him toward the guilt, resignation, and anxiety extreme of behavior.

4. *"Industry versus inferiority"* (middle childhood). The child learns to win recognition by producing things. The danger at this stage lies in a sense of inadequacy or inferiority. If he despairs of his tools and skills or his status among his peers, the child's ego boundary suffers and he abandons hope of early identification with his peers. This is what happens to the youngster whose science project was not good enough to be exhibited in the science fair, or to the child who sings too poorly to be in the church youth choir?

5. *"Ego identity versus role diffusion"* (adolescence). The sense of ego identity is a crude confidence that one feels when his inner feelings match those of other people and are acceptable to them. A career is a

tangible example. Adolescents who decide upon a career develop a basic confidence (ego identity) that their ideas (inner person) match society's expectations. The career may change, but they have found a comfortable niche and are not "searching" with the accompanying dissatisfaction (role diffusion).

The danger at this stage is role diffusion. Where inability to decide on a career is based on strong previous doubt about one's sexual identity, delinquency and outright psychosis are not uncommon behavior patterns. The inability to settle on an occupational identity disturbs young people. The new Boy Scout Explorer Post specialty program is based on this stage of development. Explorer Posts are now organized around career specialties such as law, medicine, and so on.

6. *"Intimacy versus isolation"* (early adulthood). To emerge from individual identity and fall completely in love or join a cause that involves sharing fully with others is "intimacy." The avoidance of such experiences because of the fear of ego loss may lead to a deep sense of isolation and subsequent self-absorption. For a fuller explanation of love, Erikson tells us that the "Utopia of Love" should include a mutuality of organism with a love partner of the opposite sex, with whom one is willing to share mutual trusts, to regulate the cycles of work, procreation, and recreation, and so to secure satisfactory development to the offspring. Such a utopian accomplishment cannot be an individual or, indeed, a therapeutic task; neither is it a purely sexual matter.

7. *"Generativity versus ego stagnation"* (middle adulthood). Generativity is primarily interest in establishing and guiding the next generation, a parental kind of responsibility. Where parental enrichment fails, a regression from generativity to an obsessive need for pseudointimacy often takes place, with a pervading sense of individual stagnation and interpersonal impoverishment. The individual who is totally tied up in his work or who has reached a plateau and is bored and searching for a new challenge has reached ego stagnation.

8. *"Ego integrity versus despair"* (late adulthood). Although he is aware of the relativity of the various lifestyles which have given meaning to human striving, the individual who possesses ego integrity is ready to defend the dignity of his lifestyle against physical and economic threats. The lack of accrued ego integration is signified by a fear of death. If the individual fears that his lifestyle is not accepted as the ultimate pattern, he will despair. He feels that time is too short for him to attempt to start another life and to try alternate roads to ego integrity.

Identify each of Erickson's stages of development with an age level.
Place yourself along the continuum of development. Try to identify
the age at which you passed through each of the stages.

You may have difficulty analyzing yourself, but you can more easily identify your friends' and acquaintances' stages of development. Try to place someone you know in each of the stages of development. You can see how each stage would generally fit a particular age group. For example, the senior author of this book cannot remember when he passed the first stage, trust versus distrust, but his grandson at six months has developed a strong trust, making baby-sitting for him easy. Number two, the stage of A friend's nine-month-old daughter is in the stage of "autonomy or shame and doubt," feeding herself and expressing her likes and dislikes. These may be examples of early development; experience tells us that infants do not progress in a single direction at an even rate. When the grandson is a year old, he may cry furiously when his mother leaves him with a babysitter, but later he will again accept her departure peacefully. All development progresses in fits and spurts with plateaus and differing rates of change.

Effective recreation program professionals, responsible for a neighborhood center, must gather a great deal of information about their neighborhood. Decisions on the inclusion, exclusion, or development of certain leisure activities depend upon the professional's analysis of neighborhood needs. He must know the total population; the number in each age group; the number of families; the number of families with only one parent; what type of housing is most common; the educational economic, and health status of the people; the crime rate; and the geographical barriers (lakes, highways, factories) before he can make decisions about specific programs.

Certain groups with special needs must be taken into account, for example, the aging, the bedridden, and the young mothers. All groups need activities that meet their particular needs and are effective in improving the quality of life of group members.

As a professional recreator, you may be in charge of a neighborhood that is in the midst of change. Changing neighborhoods require even more study and analysis than stable ones. You must identify the direction of the change and select recreation programs to promote that change, *if it is for the better.* Conversely, if the neighborhood is changing for the worse, you must develop programs to reverse the change.

It is often difficult to obtain such detailed information about your community. If you cannot get complete information, the best and perhaps the simplest way to begin is to identify the age groups in the neighborhood and to develop your program according to the characteristics of each group.

The organization of society affects our developmental patterns. We live in an age of urbanization, a fact which dictates many of the interrelationships of family units, of neighbors, and of groups of people to other groups. The next few pages summarize the authors' observations of age groups. The observations are broad, comprehensive, and conglomerate, and only indicate the depth of possible analysis. They include some statistical information concerning such items as divorce rates, delinquency, health statistics, and organization of the educational system. Generally they reflect middle-class America. Progression from one age group to another is identified by behavioral characteristics; therefore, these groups are delineated not only by age but also by social units such as school grade levels.

AGE OF BABYHOOD: 0–3 YEARS

The first two years of our lives involve fairly rapid change. Physical growth is rapid; birthweight doubles by five months and triples within a year. At six months the appearance of teeth changes the baby's eating habits from a liquid diet to a soft and then a regular diet. At approximately a year, the toddler becomes a walker and explores many new places. He must be constantly supervised so that his climbing experience is safe. He widens his horizon from the nursery to the entire house and the yard. At two years he begins to talk. He can communicate many things before this time, but he actually puts sentences together at two years. His communication improves and he understands and can develop some reasoning ability, conversing not only with his parents, but also with his peers and others.

PRESCHOOLERS: 4 AND 5 YEARS

From three to five years the child progressively practices his skills at large-muscle activities. The games he plays, involving shapes, sizes, colors, body parts, and recognition of dangerous situations, are all part of the growing-up process begun during babyhood.

The child develops his personal living skills in the self-centered world of babyhood. As he gains skills, he is also faced with the necessity of sharing with others. His parents probably expand his contacts by gradually exposing him to other groups, such as the church nursery group or a friend's children. His horizon of acquaintances and situations broadens. Placing the child in a nursery school or a preschool situation is considered by many parents to be very important. Studies indicate that this is a key age is setting attitudes and developing the basic concepts that will guide the individual throughout the rest of his life. The old saying of the Church, "Give me the child for the first seven years of his life and he will be mine forever," has a great deal of basic truth.

THE DRAMATIC AGE: GRADES 1 AND 2

During the dramatic age children are the greatest mimics in the world. What they observe, they act out. They live in the land of make-believe. The teacher will learn from the talkative youngster everything that goes on in the household. Conversely, the teacher has few secrets from her students, who tell their parents all they know. Youngsters at this age have a short interest span, approximately twenty minutes. They want to participate; each must have equal time. Praise is a great motivator. Learning to read opens the wide world of books to them.

TRANSITIONAL: GRADE 3

During the transitory third grade, individual change is most evident. Some children are still functioning at the first-and second-grade level, while others have progressed to the fourth-and fifth-grade level. They are no longer in awe of the school or the teacher after attending school for two years; they want to express themselves and they often do things they know are wrong.

THE INQUISITIVE AGE: GRADES 4 AND 5

At this age level the true scientist is born. The child continually questions why? why? why? He is no longer satisfied with Santa Claus and the stork, but wants logical answers. Even though his basis for belief and his factual information are slim, he demands a logical, simple explanation of why things happen.

THE IDEALIST AGE: MIDDLE SCHOOL—
GRADES 6, 7, and 8

The child now becomes an inquisitive "idealist," whose questions are replaced by a desire to see ideas at work. Grades 6, 7 and 8 are now called middle school rather than junior high school to reflect the concept that school at that age does not mimic high school but involves a separate age group with unique characteristics. At this stage children encounter problems of working out ideas in a practical way. They are very conscious of puberty and body changes. Girls are ahead of boys in development. Children are also greatly interested in the social structure of society. Girls wonder how soon they can wear lipstick; boys notice the girls, but will have little to do with them.

GRADES 9 AND 10: 15 AND 16 YEARS

The youngsters are now freshmen and sophomores in high school. There is a difference in the developmental maturity of boys and girls. Many girls are dating older boys, even seniors. At this stage youths seek independence; perhaps their biggest motivation is to show that they are self-sufficient. Many rebel at attending school, because the law in most states requires them to attend until they are sixteen or have finished ninth grade. They must belong to a peer group, whose wishes are strong motivators. Peer group demands are often set ahead of parental requests. The youngsters must try every fad. They wish to be considered and treated as adults, yet they lack the skills necessary to compete in the adult world.

GRADES 11 AND 12: 17 AND 18 YEARS

The differences between ninth and tenth grades and eleventh and twelfth grades seems to revolve around the youngster's ability to gain a set of wheels. One's own transportation visibly supports one's independence. Many states give learners' permits which license the student at an earlier age, but he cannot drive without an adult. He frets until he is eligible for and receives parental and legal permission to drive by himself. Independent transportation seems to make a great difference in his attitude toward life.

The male's independent transportation gives impetus to dating. Until this time he has been dependent upon his parents, older siblings, or older friends to furnish transportation for "double-dating."

Late teenagers are given (or perhaps more accurately, they assume) more latitude in governing their lives. They appreciate certain rules and boundaries, especially if they have some say in determining those boundaries. They exercise much control over their activities. Most youths at this age are very concerned about their careers.

Graduation from high school represents a definite turning point. Now the youth must decide to go on to school, to seek a career, or to enter the armed services.

An old saying goes, "If you want to know anything, ask a high school senior; he has all the answers." Many are bored with public school. They are approaching a change, and they wish to activate the change as soon as possible.

ADULT GROUPS

The median age for high school graduates is nineteen. The graduate's life style changes abruptly upon leaving school. An increasing percentage of high school graduates are continuing their education in junior college. Nationally, 57 percent go on to some form of higher education.

We consider as adults those people over eighteen years of age, realizing that this is an arbitrary classification attempting to describe a gradual transition. The most discerning factor is marriage, not age or whether the individual is in school, working, or a member of the armed services. Other sociological factors considered in grouping people as adults include the following:

The average age at marriage is twenty for females, twenty-two for males.

The divorce rate is one out of four, peaking at the first, fifth, tenth, and twentieth years of marriage.

The average American family has 2.4 children.

Over 40 percent of American females work, and the percentage is increasing.

We average three major career changes during our lifetime and change jobs five to seven times.

We move, changing geographical location, an average of five times during our lives.

YOUNG ADULTS

Consider an "average" couple: they marry at twenty, have their first child at twenty-two and a second at twenty-four. Six years later both children are in school and the couple is thirty years old. By the time the couple reach thirty-eight, their children are in middle school and high school, and by age of forty-two, the children have graduated from high school.

There is evidence of high incidence of career change during the first and second years of employment, and again in about five years. The critical periods for change in career are at thirty, again at forty, and once again at fifty-five.

We grouped children with similar characteristics according to two-year spans, but adults have a slower rate of change and can be grouped in longer time spans. People at the following ages seem to have similar characteristics: 20–25, 26–30, 31–36, 37–45, 46–54, 55–65, 66–75, 76 and older.

Young Single Adults: 19 to 25 Years

The characteristics of single junior college and university graduates in the working force and singles in the armed services are very similar. There is a definite change in the attitude toward this group of parents, school authorities, armed forces personnel, and supervisors on the job. Members of this group are allowed to make decisions with fewer guidelines and fewer definite boundaries.

The major motivation for this age group remains that of belonging to and identifying with a particular person or small group. Identification may take the form of seeking a mate for life (man–woman relationship) or of being directly involved in a cause. Either exemplifies the sixth stage of Erickson's continuum, "Intimacy versus isolation." If the individual did not go on to college, he may become deeply interested in a "career cause." He wants to identify with the work force and will try diligently to learn the intricacies of his business or process. If involvement is not possible at work, he will turn to social or church groups within his community.

Young Married Adults: 20 to 25 Years

The young adult who has found a mate assumes different characteristics from singles of the same age. During the first two years of marriage, couples are trying each other out, finding and developing satisfying intimate relationships. They tend to develop intimacy and companionship with each other to the exclusion of outsiders. Young married couples generally seek other young couples' company on occasion, but are not active members of groups because they are primarily interested in their dual relationship.

The advent of the first child changes the twosome into a threesome, and the parents become very concerned about their offspring. This pattern generally corresponds to Erickson's stage of "generativity." The shift from concern about each other to the concern about their offspring makes a major difference in the household. There is a difference in the motivation of the male and the female, the female tending to rank the safety and development of the child first. The male usually share's his wife's concern, but he seems equally if not more concerned that his career develop as it should because of his added responsibilities.

26 TO 30 YEARS

The male has the strongest motivation for creating and doing whatever he can to promote his career. If a management course would improve his skills and gain him a promotion, he takes the course. His main motivation is to get ahead at work. The female, on the other hand, is concerned about her child and her home. She is probably tied to her home with two preschoolers and is busy chauffeuring, keeping house, and tending the children during most of the waking hours. This is a twenty-four-hour-a-day, seven-day-a-week job which becomes very tedious at times. There is a great demand among such women for relief from the four walls of the home. This demand is recognized by some recreation departments, which provide nurseries to allow young mothers to escape home and child and do something different for a few hours.

31 TO 36 YEARS

The husband is still concerned about his career and usually must choose whether to make a move. This period of his life often signifies the start of his second career; he is concerned over his success (or failure) after ten years on the job. His wife, on the other hand, now has all the children in school; and at this stage she finds herself with much more time on her hands. She is concerned about her personal development, too. If she has had training or schooling, she wonders whether she should enter or reenter the job market. About 40 percent of American women shift from the child-centered home to the work-centered world. Couple this with the ten-year peak divorce rate, the problems attending the male's change in careers, and perhaps a move to a new locality, and it becomes a particularly critical period in the life of the family.

37 TO 45 YEARS

In the vicinity of forty years the male faces a real problem in terms of his being able to find another position because of competition from younger men. If he has delayed his second career move until forty, he probably will not change careers until semiretirement. A strong feeling of security is important.

Most males have not been overly concerned with their health or physical attractiveness for the past twenty years. Now the male begins to look at the scale and to keep his physical examination appointments. A few of his friends die of heart attacks. He may now be referred to as Mr. Blank and not Bill Blank, or he may overhear a pretty secretary refer to him as "old Mr. Blank." He recognizes that time is flying by, and he does things to prove he is still young. Sports car sales and health club memberships sold to this age group are mute evidence of these concerns.

Women in this age group who have not returned to the labor market with the accompanying satisfaction of job responsibilities become highly involved in church work, women's club work, and other community affairs. This is also the age when most couples, if they have not already joined a country club or other social club, will seriously consider doing so.

46 TO 54 YEARS

Forty-six to fifty-five is the main age in which the battle to remain young and the desire for new experiences become strong forces opposing the need for continued security by not changing or taking chances.

Women in this age group are going through menopause. Even though modern medicine has greatly eased this change, they are still very concerned about loss of femininity, changes in sexual behavior and desires, and changes in family relationships. Men, too, undergo a change of life which, though physically not as evident as menopause, also brings psychological and emotional changes.

Whatever career decision the male made at forty, he is now committed to live with it until he is fifty-five, which is usually the earliest retirement date with pension. Younger men (and women) are pushing hard, and careers require a great deal of time and energy at a period when it would be easier to taper off a bit. Interesting, constructive leisure activities are of great concern to this group, in preparation for retirement, but also to ease the tensions so prevalent at this time of life.

55 TO 65 YEARS

About age fifty-five another factor influences the lives of both husband and wife: their offspring become independent of them, and they seek to reestablish companionship. They become very aware of retirement and the preparation they should make for it during the next five or ten years. Early retirement plans in federal and armed services have created a large and growing group of fifty-five-to sixty-five-year-old retirees. Many couples plan and take longer trips, for they now have more money, having reached their maximum income at a time when family responsibilities have lessened. If there is to be a change in a career, this may be is the time for it—when only two people are taking the chance. The divorce rate at this stage is very high, probably because of the lessened responsibilities of children and the added desire for a change. Another big factor is health: both individuals are concerned about their physical appearances, but more so about their possibilities of having heart attacks, arthritis, or any other crippling disease that could leave them semi-invalid or dependent upon others after all these years of independence.

66 TO 75 YEARS

The turning point at age sixty-five has been recognized for some time because of the social security system, adopted in 1936. The biggest motivating factor for members of this age group is having a purpose for life. They have accomplished many things, but for many of them retirement is mandatory and their jobs—their former purpose in life—is taken away. Their children are grown and are no longer dependent upon them. Their employers are making way for the younger generation. They are concerned over whether their savings will last them for the rest of their life. They are also concerned about their health.

If they have been working regular, long hours, people at this stage have a tedious task ahead. To change their mode of life, retiring to a leisure-centered world with excessive amounts of free time, requires a major psychological reversal.

76 YEARS AND OVER

About 10 percent of the population of the United States is already or soon will be seventy-six. In fact, ten thousand Americans are one hundred or more years old. The number of people in this age group is increasing as we find ways of keeping people physically young and postponing old-age deficiencies.

Some of these people need nursing-home care because of poor health. Others are simply existing, concerned primarily about continuing life easily. Many may lead very active lives.

SUMMARY

The characteristics of the age categories described above have been a broad conglomeration of many factors; it is difficult to specify age and developmental patterns at any particular time of life. However, we all experience the various stages of development at our individual rates. It is therefore important to recognize the sociological factors of divorce, delinquency, health statistics, and so on when planning leisure activities for groups of people.

Suggested Reading

BIRREN, JAMES E., "Psychological Aspects of Aging: Intellectual Functioning," *The Gerontologist,* VIII, Part II (1968), 16–19.

BISCHOF, LEDFORD J., *Adult Psychology.* New York: Harper and Row, Publishers, 1969.

DODSON, FITZHUGH, *How to Parent.* New York: Nash Publishing Corp., 1970.

ERIKSON, ERIC H., *Childhood and Society* (rev. ed.). New York: W. W. Norton & Company, Inc., 1964.

FARINA, A. J., " A Study of the Relationships Between Personality Factors and Patterns of Freetime Behavior," *Dissertation Abstracts,* XXVI (1966), 4795–96.

HAVIGHURST, ROBERT J., *"Personality and Patterns of Aging," The Gerontologist,* VIII, Part II (1968), 20–23.

JERSILD, ARTHUR T., *Child Psychology* (5th ed.). Englewood Cliffs, N.J.: Prentice-Hall, Inc., 1968.

chapter four

THE ROLE OF
LEISURE - RECREATION
IN SATISFYING
MAN'S NEEDS

Absence of occupation is not rest.

WILLIAM COWPER

Men always want something to do. They simply cannot sit and do nothing for any extended period of time. The number and variety of possible activities are almost endless; there are more than one hundred ways to play Bingo! Recreation activity programs have grown so much that the time has come to sort them out and to guide each community to provide opportunities for its citizens to participate in activities that contribute to their development.

SELECTION OF ACTIVITIES

How do we select the proper activities to contribute to our developmental needs at each stage? Individuals make decisions for themselves, but most people are greatly influenced by close friends and experts. If you as a professional expert in leisure are to influence people's choices of leisure activity, you should examine motivation studies.

Applying this knowledge to leadership principles will help you to educate people for leisure living. The job of the leisure-recreation professional is to prepare and furnish materials for all leisure programs.

> *What activities would you suggest for your father and/or mother? Explain your choices.*

Every program, no matter how big or small, must be completely thought out. A written proposal must be presented to the authorities. Some departments or companies term this process "formation of a plan of action" or "determining the critical path." The proposal must contain all the factors in detail. It must contain objectives and goals; the number, description, and location of people to be served; a time schedule for each item; an enumeration of facilities and supplies needed; a description of the leadership involved; and a reliable cost estimate of the operation. When the authorities review and approve the plan, target dates for its sequential development must be fixed and a series of periodic evaluation procedures added to assure quality performance. Attention to details in the planning stage avoids problems in operation. New factors that develop as a project progresses should be added at the periodic review or evaluation.

> *Select an activity you think a department or company should sponsor. Make a "plan of action" to present to the authorities.*

ORGANIZATION OF MATERIALS

A part of educating people for leisure is the preparation of varied motivational materials for each leisure program sponsored by a professional recreation leader. For example, if you sponsor a boys' baseball program, you would set up a series of motivational events aimed at interesting the boys in baseball—announce tryouts, design special T-shirts and caps, have a prominent baseball figure (a big-league hero) make appearances, and so on.

> *How would you promote participation in a girls' softball league, teen clubs, square dancing, a senior citizens' club?*

Accompanying your promotional campaign should be materials aimed at the parents—pamphlets, lectures, meetings, endorsements, and so on. This information should contain a simple explanation of the purposes, goals, organizational details, and responsibilities of parents, boys or girls, coaches, and department. People want to know why their boy (girl) and his friends should participate, as well as how the program is run. A mother wants to know, "Is Little League good for my boy?" You probably answer "yes" because of your personal love of the game and because baseball involves a great deal of publicity and community appeal. However, the professional recreator will help the mother reach her decision by furnishing material that explains why he sponsors the program in enough detail to guide her appraisal of her son and to determine the appropriateness of the activity for his developmental stage. The material should contain the following minimum information:

Purpose—goals. Be specific; avoid claiming too many possible benefits. For example, explain that your program will (1) improve the player's physical skills (throwing, catching, and so on), and (2) improve the player's self-concept and confidence.

Organization details. Give the schedule, the field, dates of tournaments; list postseason possibilities. Detail the costs and explain who bears them. Give procedures for injuries and accidents. List special rules concerning equal playing time, choice of all-stars, how teams select players, absence, tardiness, code of behavior for parents and players.

Personal readiness. Include a chart of normal age, height, weight; detail basic physical skills needed, such as throw, catch, run, bat. Ask whether the boy wants to play or his parents want him to; determine his other interests and hobbies, and whether they will leave time for his participation.

Family involvement. Who provides transportation to field? Should parents attend games? How should families react to players' success or failure? Will there be interference with family schedules—meals, vacation? What happens if a player wants to drop out, go swimming instead of practice, and so on? How much home help will be necessary to help the player practice skills?

> *Make a brochure for parents explaining why you sponsor a specific program. Choose any activity and try to involve different age groups. For example: (1) girls 6–9 years, ballet program; (2) teen drama group; (3) senior citizens' forum; (4) ceramics; (5) day camp; (6) women's auto mechanics; (7) city band.*

Your program materials should reflect a knowledge of the individual development process. Is the boy in Erikson's fourth stage, "industry versus inferiority"? (See Chapter Three.) Is he seeking to win recognition by producing? To produce, he must be big enough to swing a bat and have enough eye–hand coordination to catch and throw accurately. If he does not possess enough skill to compete with his peers, his productivity will be low and failure will increase his feeling of inferiority. If so, he really is not ready for your program. Does the boy himself want to play, or is playing his mother's or father's idea? Parents are vitally concerned about their children and need guidance in evaluating leisure activities. All departments should furnish program material aimed at furnishing answers to the question, "Why participate?"

Examine your baseball program closely. Is its organizational pattern based on its purposes and goals? Are boys ten, eleven, and twelve years old on the same team? If so, does the ten-year-old play at all? Does he have equal chance to produce the hits, runs, and fielding plays that gain recognition from his peers? Do you yourself preach fair play, while your coaches emphasize winning at any cost? The answers call for forthright evaluation. Parents have a right to know your professional opinion; they will be guided by materials you furnish, and by their discoveries in response to your questions.

> *Make a checklist of questions about each program to guide evaluation of that program. What do you need to know to determine whether to continue, change, or delete a program?*

Although our example was a youth physical program, baseball, the same general treatment should be followed for every program: art, music, drama, debate, nature, camping, and so on. This is also true for adult-centered programs. People need a reason and a purpose for participation. The reason must be valid enough to the individual to stimulate his participation. Adults recommend programs to each other; give everyone the materials for guiding his friends.

For too long we have looked only at the physical development of individuals. We have disseminated enough information that the general public is now aware of its physical capabilities and recognizes the outward signs of physical development. We have also published the techniques of playing various games and physical activities. The many pseudocoaches in the stands have come to believe that they can coach a team or direct individual play in diverse physical activities.

However, little attention has been given to human psychology. Today's leisure-recreation leaders must understand man's psychological as well as his physical development. It is difficult to separate the psychological, physical, intellectual, and religious sides of people. Actually, we should not try to separate them; we should treat the individual as a whole person. Each aspect of physical development is related to psychological development in a sophisticated and intricate pattern. That we understand man's total development and aim our leisure activities to his continued development is of paramount importance. Our institutions for the mentally ill are filled with people who have grown up with low and underdeveloped "leisure quotients." Fortunately, few damaged personalities have resulted from a professional recreation leader's inability to prescribe positive leisure pursuits. Countless individuals, however, bear the scars of bad experiences. Sound professional know-how is needed to undo as well as to avoid recurring negative experiences.

LEADERSHIP

The biggest factor in any program is leadership; to build a team of professionals with supporting technical, paraprofessional, and other workers is a never-ending job that requires great insight into people. It is not our objective to give the details of personnel recruitment, selection, placement, in-service training, promotion, evaluation, and dismissal practices. However, you should recognize and understand some of the ideas and the scope of the task of personnel management for recreation programs.

Leaders are required at all levels of recreation programming. The skills, techniques, and background needed for each position must be determined. Studies indicate that we can group personnel roughly into four functional units:

1. *Superintendent.* Interprets program to the public.
   Assistant Superintendent. (in large departments). Organizes communication within the department.
2. *Supervisor.* Encourages, develops, and guides programs.
3. *Director.* Coordinates all programs in a prescribed area or center.
4. *Worker.* Is a face-to-face or group stimulator to motivate and guide participants.

The duties and responsibilities of each individual must be determined. There are two distinct types of leadership techniques: the *autocratic approach,* in which the leader determines policy, establishes goals, assigns tasks and, in general, dominates the group; and the *demo-*

cratic approach, in which the group determines policy, establishes goals, accepts tasks and, in general, cooperates and shares leadership. The use of one technique or the other depends on the goals of the program.

Principles of Leadership

Howard Danford has listed sixteen principles of leadership that are most helpful in designing a plan of action to influence people in participating in meaningful leisure activity:[1]

1. Leadership must be based upon a sound philosophy of recreation.
2. Leadership is dedicated to the principle of involvement.
3. Effective leadership depends in large measure upon the leader's insight into the nature of man and his behavior.
4. Leadership functions in harmony with the principle of individual differences.
5. Leadership is shaped and fashioned both by the group and by the situation.
6. Compatibility must exist between means and ends.
7. Leadership establishes an organizational structure for effective operation.
8. The effectiveness of leadership is measured by the degree to which it attains its goals.
9. Leadership seeks a compromise between the extremes of individualism and equalitarianism.
10. Leadership accepts responsibilities and risks.
11. Leadership operates in harmony with the principle of multiple choices.
12. Leadership seeks to expand the interests of people.
13. Extreme discrepancies between the intelligence of potential leaders and their followers militate against the exercise of leadership.
14. Leadership anticipates difficulties before they arise and acts to prevent them.
15. Leadership attempts to realize as large a return as possible on all facilities, activities, and services.
16. Leadership is based on continuous evaluation.

Theories of Leadership

The education of professional recreation leaders involves the basic behavioral sciences, such as psychology and sociology. Leaders will differ

[1]Howard G. Danford, *Creative Leadership in Recreation* (Boston: Allyn & Bacon, Inc., 1970). pp. 93–103.

depending on their concept of behavior. For example, the *environmental view* of behavior emphasizes that man is at the mercy of his environment. An environmental behaviorist concentrates on surrounding individuals with an environment that will stimulate and influence them to perceive themselves and their environment. He develops skill in manipulating the proper forces at the proper times to achieve what has been accepted as proper behavior. Many traditional activities have been established and promoted because of this concept of behavior. Build a pleasant park with green lawns, shade trees, bicycle trails, and playing fields, and people will use them. Open the swimming pool during warm weather. The environmental surroundings motivate all those within reach to participate.

The *perceptual view* of behavior holds that man is not completely at the mercy of his environment; he controls at least part of his destiny. How he sees himself and his world is a personal matter. You cannot *make* people perceive or *force* them to change concepts. Man is not open to direct manipulation; leaders must use persuasion, understanding, and recognition of mutual goals and concepts to provide recreation experiences that contribute to success and self-assurance. The perceptual view values highly the skill of the leader in a one-to-one or small-group relationship.

Both concepts should be used in a total recreation-parks system. Recreation activity planning for the whole community could be environmentally oriented, resulting in a system offering many varied experiences to the public. Choice of activity would be left to the individual; motivation would come from extrinsic incentives, such as ribbons for a swim meet. The system should also provide perceptually-oriented leaders who could guide and influence those persons having difficulties in selecting activities that would fulfill developmental needs.

You as professional recreator select a staff to organize and conduct the various programs. You will become aware of three generally recognized theories of leadership. The *trait* theory is based on the assumption that leaders are born, not made, exhibiting certain traits that were originally thought to be innate. Later theorists agreed that such traits may be acquired through education, experiences, or special training. Studies have shown that trait theory is not valid. Leadership as a *group function,* in which a group assists in establishing and achieving goals, is a second recognized theory. Leadership in this instance does not center on one person, but resides in the group. Members of the group perform different functions. All members are potential leaders and exhibit leadership to some degree. Leadership as a *situational function* is the third theory. A leader in one group does not necessarily function as a leader in another. Leadership qualities are related to the situation, for example, a football team captain may not be a leader in the classroom. The leader must be superior to others in respect to the goal to be achieved—stronger if the task demands strength, more verbal if the task demands persuasion, and so on.

> *Design an application form for recreation personnel. Will one form do for all positions? Design an interview guide and rating sheet that would help you select the best qualified from a large group of prospects. Selection of the right personnel is the key to success.*

EDUCATION OF RECREATION PROFESSIONALS

A recreation leader who knows a little about organization technique but does not know all the implications of an activity and its effect on personal development may be an asset to some mass programs, but here, as in other fields, a little learning is usually a dangerous thing. Too often recreation leaders with good technical knowledge of program skills but little knowledge of behavioral science are made professional program directors, with dire results. A program technician is relatively easy to produce, but a true professional leader needs extensive education.

Most recreation leaders inherit programs and are slow to analyze them critically for strengths and weaknesses in terms of developmental aspects and opportunities for the community. They tend to introduce and promote programs that seem to be popular and only incidentally contribute to individual development. Too often, programs are developed primarily by a hit-and-miss process. We do not know exactly why we are sponsoring an activity; its success or failure is based solely on attendance. Much more information than that is needed for effective recreation programming.

Over the past one hundred years various agencies have assumed responsibility for directing the leisure of Americans. They have identified areas of concern and promoted programs to fill basic leisure needs. Many of these programs have kept up with changing needs, while others have become stereotyped, held back by the dead hand of tradition. Many of the programs of ten years ago have changed measurably in aim, organization, and activity although they still have the traditional name, emblem, motto, and so on. One of the biggest problems we face is that of cooperation among agencies to avoid unnecessary duplication of effort in a community where needs far exceed the combined efforts of all. The following chapters are aimed at describing the main agencies and their efforts to meet the leisure needs of people in our communities.

Design a model curriculum for (1) a recreation activity leader, (2) a recreation center director, (3) a recreation program supervisor (over several centers), (4) a superintendent of recreation for a town of 50,000 people.

Selected Reading

BRIGHTBILL, CHARLES K., *The Challenge of Leisure.* Englewood Cliffs, N.J.: Prentice-Hall, Inc., 1963.

CORBIN, H. DAN, *Recreation Leadership* (3rd ed.). Englewood Cliffs, N.J.: Prentice-Hall, Inc., 1970.

DANFORD, HOWARD G., *Creative Leadership in Recreation.* Boston: Allyn & Bacon, Inc., 1970.

GORDON, SOL, and RISA S. GOLOB, *Recreation and Socialization for the Brain-Injured Child.* East Orange, N.J.: New Jersey Association for Brain-Injured Children, Central New Jersey Section, 1966.

HAVIGHURST, ROBERT, "The Leisure Activities of the Middle-Aged," *Journal of Sociology,* LXIII (September 1957).

KELLY, JOHN R., "Work and Leisure: A Simplified Paradigm," *Journal of Leisure Research,* IV (Winter 1972).

LARRABEE, ERIC, and ROLF MEYERSOHN, eds., *Mass Leisure.* New York: The Free Press, 1958.

MEYER, HAROLD D., CHARLES K. BRIGHTBILL, and H. DOUGLAS SESSOMS, *Community Recreation: A Guide to its Organization.* Englewood Cliffs, N.J.: Prentice-Hall, Inc., 1969.

O'MORROW, GERALD S., "The Whys of Recreation Activities for Psychiatric Patients," *Therapeutic Recreation Journal,* V, no. 3 (1971).

SHIVERS, JAY S., *Leadership in Recreational Service.* New York: The Macmillan Company, 1963.

" CALCULATING THE CURVILINEAR LINE **WITHOUT**
THE COMPUTER, ALVIN, DETERMINE THE DISTANCE
OF YOUR DRIVE, PLEASE. "

chapter five

THE SCHOOL
AND EDUCATION
FOR LEISURE

*The great secret of education is to make the
exercises of the body and of the mind
always serve as a recreation for each other.*

JEAN ROUSSEAU

Essentially, the school is an institution dedicated to the task of passing from one generation to the next the social heritage of the human race. It deals with the fundamentals of man's accumulated knowledge and attempts to guide the individual's adjustment to the world about him. The school has accepted as one of its responsibilities the education of the individual in the worthy use of leisure time. This was officially recognized when the National Education Association in 1918 accepted the report of its Commission on the Reorganization of Secondary Education, establishing the Seven Cardinal Principles of Education, which emphasized the worthy use of leisure as one of its major objectives.

How best to reach the individual is a logical concern of the educator. It is acknowledged that children are most self-revealing during play. They are most impressionable and teachable when they are doing what is most satisfying and challenging to them. Consequently, a competent leisure-recreation leader can be a powerful force, both uncovering that which is best and detecting faulty behavior tendencies in their early stages, thereby avoiding their further development.

Education for leisure is a communitywide responsibility embracing home, school, and all the other community influences. It is highly desirable that the school be considered as one place where satisfying recreational experiences occur. The use of a recreational approach toward academic learning is to be encouraged. In *Crisis in the Classroom,* Charles Silberman laments "the sharp but wholly artificial dichotomy between work and play which schools create and maintain."[1]

EDUCATION FOR LEISURE

The function of schools in providing recreation education is vitally significant. It will play a leading part in determining whether man will survive the products of his inventions. We must examine critically what has been and is being done in the field, with a view to correcting past and present errors and providing every means for the achievement of our goals.

The responsibilities of teachers will vary. We must expect competent leadership from teachers certified in elementary and secondary education and the special fields of physical education, music, language arts, drama, art, and handicrafts. Do these teachers fulfill their responsibilities? Have they been prepared for this particular phase of their work? Can we expect efficient work if the requirements for certification do not include adequate preparation in education for leisure?

PROFESSIONAL PREPARATION OF TEACHERS

Physical education requirements in the curricula for the professional preparation of elementary and secondary teachers are woefully weak. The fields of music, language arts, drama, and art should include

---

[1]Charles E. Silberman, *Crisis in the Classroom* (New York: Random House, Inc., 1970), p. 141.

education for leisure. Milton Gabrielsen reminds us; "Part of the fault lies with the failure of teachers of subject areas to recognize the potentials of their subjects as leisure-time activities. This situation could be improved by the introduction, at the teacher training level, of courses interpreting the implications of leisure for education and by a careful analysis of each subject area to discover its potential contribution as a leisure-time activity."[2]

Those who defend the practices followed in the professional preparation of teachers in the special areas of education point out that material on education for leisure is included in other courses. This is true to a limited degree, but emphasis in such courses has been placed upon the perfection of performance rather than upon enjoyment of performance. When graduates of such courses enter the field of teaching, their methods are bound to be directed toward perfection rather than enjoyment.

THE FIELD OF MUSIC

The family often contributes generously toward the musical background of its members, but to rely on it exclusively as a source of musical instruction would be foolhardy, and comparable to relegating the teaching of art to the home. In essence, the contribution of the family is to make available to the school a more advanced and highly impressionable youngster.

Music education consists of several major areas of achievement:

1. Enjoyment and appreciation as a listener
2. Some proficiency as a performer
3. Artistry of performance
4. Ability in the art of composition
5. Ability to teach and direct others

Naturally, our abilities vary; some of us accomplish all of these desirable outcomes, while others hardly scratch the surface in even one area.

A professor of music at a leading university pinpointed the problem:

[2]Milton A. Gabrielsen, "What Is the Role of the School in Recreation?" *Recreation Magazine*, XLVII, No. 7 (September 1955), p. 328.

"The trouble with our school of music is that it spends 95 percent of its time and effort upon composition and concert performance and 5 percent upon pedagogy; yet the vast majority will enter the teaching field. Those teaching after the first year will have a suitcase full of questions to which they wish they had answers." If these teachers have had only 5 percent of their instructional emphasis on pedagogy, what a small percentage must have been on education for leisure in the field of music!

Courses in music appreciation seem to focus on developing in the student an appreciation of what is considered good music, instead of on developing self-satisfaction through participation. We have been made to feel that our participation in vocal or instrumental music must meet the approval of others. We are afraid to sing or play for fear that we will not perform well enough; we sing in the shower, where the sound of the water drowns out our voices, but we are afraid to sing where others might hear us.

Singing is a recognized morale builder. One example is an army platoon singing on the march. The men are not concerned with vocal perfection, they sing for enjoyment and for a lift. If music is to be a vehicle in education for wholesome leisure, then music teachers must break down people's inhibitions against participating in music. They must emphasize that enjoyment and satisfaction are primary reasons for participation. Although acquiring skill is important—it helps to break down inhibitions and develop self-confidence—it must not be the sole objective.

Education for leisure should include both vocal and instrumental music. The vocal program should include group singing, choruses, glee clubs, quartets, singing games, folk songs, and so on. The instrumental program should include not only bands and orchestras, which are generally limited to the better musicians, but also rhythm bands, harmonica bands, comb bands, and playing the cigarbox fiddle and musical saw. Strumming the ukulele is fun and easily learned. These activities lend themselves to satisfying and exhilarating musical experience.

They build the realization that music is fun and that everyone, not just a talented few can take part. "Less stress is placed on excellence, although skillful performance need not be ruled out as a phase of recreational music. Although effective performance may be sought, it need not be at the expense of the satisfactions which should be uppermost in the minds of recreation personnel; the joys of singing or playing are of prime importance, with technical excellence to be relegated to a minor role."[3]

Participation in instrumental or vocal music usually leads to a greater enjoyment and appreciation of music, perhaps even to active participation in instrumental or vocal forms of expression. Musical interests of individuals can grow and expand so that the entire community benefits.

> It is in our free time that we can wriggle out now and then into some manner of life that is more than of individual importance. I remember a friend, a business man, who played the cello, and who found pleasure in forming a quartet that played once a week in his home. But the inevitable happened. Art has a way of pushing out beyond itself; and it was not long before this man and his friends were organizing concerts for their community, bringing to it outstanding artists who otherwise would not have been heard.[4]

THE FIELD OF ART

We could also criticize the way art is taught in the schools, with perfection as the goal. Art teachers have not advocated "Paint for the joy of painting and each in his separate star paints the thing as he sees it for the God of things as they are."[5]

Several years ago Dr. Frank Lloyd of New York University was instrumental in having the Hostess House at Camp Sebago turned into an art studio where the students could paint. An instructor was there, though in a supervisory capacity only. The student merely gathered together his canvas, easel, paints, and brushes, and began painting. If he needed help he could ask the instructor for guidance. The experiment was so successful that the majority of the students at the camp took up painting. Their work was good from the standpoint of self-satisfaction, which was the purpose of the plan.

Let it be understood that we do not criticize the teaching of art and music for professional accomplishment; that is apparently being done well. We are concerned here primarily with how education for leisure

[3]H. Dan Corbin, *Recreation Leadership* (Englewood Cliffs, N.J.: Prentice-Hall, Inc., 1970), p. 236.

[4]Harry A. Overstreet, *A Guide to Civilized Leisure* (New York: W. W. Norton & Co., Inc., 1934).

[5]Rudyard Kipling, "When Earth's Last Picture Is Painted."

can be taught in the fields of art and music. In art, as in music, teaching in the elementary grades should emphasize self-satisfaction and enjoyment. We must break down the students' inhibitions. Developing skills so that satisfaction can be achieved is an aid toward this goal. Conversely, emphasis on the development of skill beyond that point tends to intensify the inhibitions of most students.

On the secondary school level more emphasis can justifiably be placed upon the development of skill, but not so much that the concept of art as a medium of self-expression and enjoyment is lost. Sketching, drawing, painting, and design are generally recognized as art forms more commonly used in education for leisure. Discussing "What is art," (Count Lev Nikolaevich Tolstoi (1828–1910) said, "Art is a human activity having for its purpose the transmission to others of the highest and best feelings to which men have risen." Overstreet illustrates how art in its broadest sense can lead in unanticipated directions.[6] He describes some Delaware farm women who met in each others' homes to participate in the arts of weaving, rug making, and pottery. Teachers were sent by the state to guide them and to "initiate them into the mysteries of color combinations and design." Aside from the joy of creating, the women also acquired a greater awareness of design and color harmony and a thirst for natural beauty. As a consequence, they inquired why their scenic highways were permitted to be obstructed by billboards and signs. After some effort, they secured the support of their husbands. Passage of an ordinance which assured the removal of the billboards from their countryside was an outgrowth of their training in art.

THE FIELD OF HANDICRAFTS

Arts and crafts are generally linked together. Art forms are an integral part of craft work, yet they are really two separate areas in education. Craft work involves construction—craftsmanship—and design—a form of art. Craft programs generally deal with such media as wood, clay, metal, leather, fiber, paper, cloth, plastics, and natural items (grass, reeds, nuts, and the like). Cameras made from sea shells and

[6]Overstreet, *Guide to Civilized Leisure.*

ashtrays made from the hoofs or horns of animals are representative of the endless number of craft products.

In our frantic era of anxieties and tensions, expression through handicrafts provides release and emotional satisfaction. Crafts are also an antidote to creeping passivity. The relationship between idle hands and an idle mind is real enough to warrant our concern.

A craft-minded person resorts automatically to reflective thinking. The problems he encounters in handicraft work often call for concentrated reading, analyzing, consulting with others, and experimental application. He widens his horizons and evolves as a wiser, happier, and more skillful person.

Crafts are accompanied by the satisfactions that grow with the advancement of skill. Excelling in a craft skill can lead to monetary returns and even new careers. And, handicraft skills carry over to later years; age rarely hampers the pursuit of these activities. They lend themselves to all-family enrichment, a vital need in our time.

Craft programs in our schools are accomplishing a great deal in education for leisure. Our recommendations for improvement include (1) expanding the program to include the various handicraft media; and (2) coordinating crafts with other departments in the school, such as the fine arts and industrial arts; the use of their facilities would enrich the crafts program.

A good craft program requires facilities, equipment, and materials. Competent leadership is an essential attribute of a diversified and creative program. With all these prerequisites, crafts can be a powerful force in satisfying basic recreation needs.

THE FIELD OF DRAMATICS

The amount of attention given to dramatics varies from school to school. Work in this area is often assigned to a teacher of English or to some other teacher who has some qualification.

The place of dramatics in a sound recreation program is well established. Opportunity for creative self-expression is an important part of dramatics. The pleasurable outcome of successful participation in drama can be the development of increased poise, self-confidence, and personality integration. The child's enthusiasm for make-believe provides a wonderful opportunity for recreational expression, but the value of dramatics is not limited to children; youth and adult benefit similarly from dramatic activities.

Dramatic offerings in most schools need to be expanded to include pantomime, creative play (dramatizing a child's idea of an experience he had), skits, festivals, play production (suitable for each grade level), puppetry, and the like. Fun, enjoyment, and satisfaction are adequate incentives for education for leisure through dramatics. The organization and administration of a dramatics program must not be regimented, but suited to the needs and interests of the students.

THE FIELD OF PHYSICAL EDUCATION

Efforts in education for leisure through physical education range from excellent to poor. In some schools the emphasis in physical education is on the development of skills, attitudes, and appreciation of activities for the enjoyment of the individual and his proper growth and development. Such curricula attempt to educate the individual through physical activity. The development of physical fitness is a desirable by-product and the development of skills a means to an end: the development of the individual as a worthy member of society, well-adjusted and secure.

Other schools make no genuine attempt at a physical education program. They superficially, if at all, comply with the requirements in physical education, conducting varsity athletic programs as a guise for fulfilling those requirements.

It is obvious that physical education can contribute a great deal toward education for leisure. Leaders in the field of physical education are striving for improvement in leisure-recreation education. All of them are interested in speeding the development of sound programs of physical education in the schools. How can this work be accomplished? The first step must involve the teacher-training institutions. Professional preparation of teachers in physical education must include recreation education. This topic may be included in the subject matter of some physical education courses but it is preferable to have a separate course in education for leisure, taught by a recreation educator.

Present school programs could be improved through the employment of a recreation educator to coordinate the physical education program and develop within the school a comprehensive program of education for leisure. He could serve as counselor or coordinator, with training in recreational philosophy, objectives, principles, and techniques. With a cooperative administration and suitable instructional emphases on the part of the teaching staff, education for leisure can thrive. The physical education teacher, the coach, the intramural director, and the teachers of art, dramatics, music, and industrial arts can help to assure the desired outcomes.

Harlan Metcalf emphasizes the importance of having a recreation educator on the school personnel staff:

> The recreation educator might be employed as a regular staff member in the larger secondary schools, or be a district supervisor of recreation education in the rural areas or smaller communities. . . . Education leaders have long recognized recreation education as a basic objective of education. This objective has frequently been stated as the worthy use of leisure. However, the schools of our country have not yet seriously accepted the full responsibility for attempting to achieve this objective in the planning and administration of their programs. In physical education in recent years there have been hopeful signs. Schools and colleges are including in their program camping, bait and fly-casting, archery, golf and other pursuits that people can and will use as long as they live. However, the school's responsibility for realizing this basic educational objective is far greater than that of the physical education program. It includes many, if not all, the other curricular subjects.[7]

Education for leisure is an important objective of the school physical education program. The program must include recreational activities for all students, and leaders must be oriented toward the desired effect upon the individual: worthy use of leisure time.

OUTDOOR EDUCATION

Outdoor education as a part of the school program is growing rapidly in popularity. Camping, hiking, gardening, nature study, nature crafts, boating, and canoeing are being included in such programs. School districts are purchasing campsites and using them for holiday

[7]Harlan G. Metcalf, "Recreation Education," *Journal of American Association of Health Physical Education and Recreation,* XXIII, No. 2 (Feb. 1952), p. 20.

outings, vacations, and summer outdoor education. The park-school (a modern school in a park setting, with facilities for educational and recreational programming) can supplement school campsites or possibly substitute for them. They afford excellent opportunities for the students to have new and inspiring experiences, develop new interests, and increase their knowledge of the great outdoors.

Authorities in the field of outdoor education agree that schools must continue to develop the outdoor programs. The eleven- or twelve-month school year would allow for a more balanced blending of outdoor education with the conventional curriculum. In addition, the camp setting is highly suitable for laboratory situations involving the fauna and flora, aesthetics of art education, astronomy, nature lore, and the hobby pursuits of rock, leaf, and butterfly collecting. The un-natural conditions of modern society increase the value of outdoor education. All ages can benefit from a deeper knowledge and appreciation of nature.

In this vein, Julian Smith highlights the many forms of outdoor education.[8]

1. Outdoor-related classroom activities and units of study using available outdoor materials and resources to enrich and extend learning opportunities. Weather study, bird and animal life, erosion and pollution, art from outdoor scenes, aquariums, rock collections are examples of the use of outdoor life and resources in the regular elementary and secondary school programs.

2. The use of the school site and other outdoor areas as laboratories to extend the classroom. Field trips and outdoor projects are used to help achieve classroom objectives and effect learnings often impossible in the bounds of four walls. The use of nature trails, study of animal and plant life near the school, observation and study of aquatic life in nearby ponds and streams, creative outdoor play areas are examples of the use of outdoor laboratories.

3. Resident outdoor schools, in which students and their teachers use camp settings for learning opportunities achieved best in a camp community and outdoor laboratory. This is one of the most sensational and effective forms of outdoor education and offers extensive opportunities for learnings centering around social living, healthful living, work experiences, outdoor skills and interests, and the application of many of the school's educational objectives and purposes. On school time and as a regular part of the curriculum, the outdoor school serves to motivate and vitalize

[8]Julian W. Smith, "Where We Have Been–Where We Are–What We Will Become," *Journal of Outdoor Education,* V, No. 1 (Fall 1970), pp. 6, 7.

learning and contributes greatly to the development of good human relationships, better understanding between students and teachers, and opportunities for democratic living. The outdoor school thus achieves a greater dimension by combining outdoor learning with active participation in problem-solving in a "child's community." The potentials for learning, aptly termed "teachable moments," in such settings are rich and almost limitless.

4. The teaching of outdoor skills, usually in physical education, recreation and club programs, and the development of attitudes and appreciations through many activities in the curriculum are important aspects of outdoor education. This aspect of outdoor education is paramount in educating a citizenry for obtaining maximum satisfactions from outdoor interests and pursuits, and in becoming responsible citizens in the protection of and improvement of our outdoor resources.

5. Work–learn experiences in outdoor areas for secondary school youth, such as the improvement of the land, forest and game management, construction of facilities, conservation projects to improve the natural environment, and learning outdoor skills and interests are challenging and effective forms of outdoor education. Somewhat reminiscent of the CCC of the 1930s, a number of school-sponsored programs of this type are proving effective, particularly for potential dropouts who do not thrive on the academic diet of the traditional secondary school.

The benefits of outdoor education are limitless.

1. A greater appreciation of the environment and its impact on our leisure-time choices.

2. An ability to relate to our environment and appreciate its contribution toward "the good life."

3. A sense of responsibility to maintain a significant portion of our environment in its natural and untampered state.

4. A desire to reverse the trend toward pollution and ecological disaster so as to provide future generations with a fit environment.

5. Acquisition of lifetime skills and appreciations.

6. An awareness of the need for aesthetic influences and serenity as neutralizing factors for high-pressured and frenetic living.

THE ROLE OF THE ELEMENTARY SCHOOL

Elementary school teachers probably have the most opportunity for recreation education of any teachers in the school program. At that stage the child is most impressionable, with a natural urge for play.

The basic skills that will give him self-confidence are most readily acquired then, but overemphasis on perfection will inhibit his further participation by robbing the activity of all enjoyment.

An excellent example of a child's positive reaction to appreciation expressed by a teacher and her parents is that of a young girl who made a clay vase. It was not symmetrical, and when standing it leaned to one side. The teacher encouraged the child to take the vase home, but she hesitated to show the vase to her father and waited with misgivings for his reaction. He asked, "Did you make this? I think it's fine; it's just fine. We'll set it up here on the mantle," which he did. Some time later the girl brought home another vase, this one symmetrically proportioned and skillfully made. Her father said, "Ah, that's fine, beautifully done." When the vase was placed on the mantle the girl said, "That first one wasn't very good, was it?" Her father answered, "Oh, yes it was; if you had not made the first one you would never have made this one." We can also be sure that had she not received encouragement through praise for her first attempt she would probably never have tried again.

The elementary school student should receive valuable help from his teachers in the special fields of music, industrial arts, dramatics, art, and physical education. It is most important that those teachers recognize the problems confronting our rapidly changing society: that basic human needs must be satisfied, that conditions of modern society make it difficult for those needs to be satisfied, and that they as teachers have a definite responsibility toward educating their pupils for meaningful leisure.

THE ROLE OF THE SECONDARY SCHOOL

Teachers of special subjects in secondary education are also responsible for education for leisure. English teachers may contribute by coordinating their teaching with the dramatics program. Reading is a valuable part of recreation; poetry, like music, contributes to enjoyment and reflective thinking. Geology offers a great opportunity for developing interests in a vital leisure-time pursuit. Many public recreation departments have staff members whose job is to organize and carry out a geology program. The study of astronomy is also rich in leisure-time opportunities. Science is full of interesting and valuable areas for individual involvement.

Education for leisure is the responsibility of teachers in all grades and areas of study. It can be successful only when teachers are qualified in philosophy and attitude to organize and conduct their programs so that education for leisure is an essential objective. By employing the recreational approach, they can enlist their pupils in a lifetime of participation and enrichment.

THE SCHOOL AND THE COMMUNITY
RECREATION PROGRAM

In addition to its duty to educate for leisure, the school is also responsible to the community to make its facilities available to the citizens and to various agencies as their needs arise.

The school plant—grounds, buildings, and equipment—were paid for by people's taxes. To the school board and school administrators the people have delegated the protection and use of the schools. They rightly expect that these facilities shall be used to their maximum in serving society. When not in use in the "required" educational program of the school, these facilities should be used for the education, development, enjoyment, and welfare of the people in the community. Opening the schools for community use—the "lighted schoolhouse" concept —has been advocated for fifty years.

Too often, principals resist and oppose the use of the school for any purpose outside their restricted educational concerns. Yet across the country large and small cities have devised working arrangements, contracting with public recreation departments for the use of the school facilities with full protection of the property and payment in full for expenses incurred. There is no valid argument against the use of school facilities for the welfare of the people during non school hours.

In some cases the schools efficiently administer the public recreation program, for example, in Milwaukee. Note, however, that a trained and qualified public recreation administrator is employed as assistant superintendent of schools to administer this program.

THE ROLE OF THE BOARD OF EDUCATION

The National Conference on School Recreation recognized the responsibility of boards of education to initiate community recreation where necessary, and to cooperate with existing agencies. Any of the following approaches are recommended:

1. The board of education administers and conducts total community recreation programs.

2. The board of education pools their funds, facilities, and resources with another government agency to jointly operate a community recreation program.
3. The board of education cooperates with another government agency by permitting school district physical facilities to be used in programs operated by the outside agency.[9]

However, the consensus seems to be that a board or commission of public recreation is generally preferable. This board should include representatives from the various institutions and agencies within the community that are responsible for the recreational welfare of the people. If no recreation department or commission exists, the school should take the initiative in seeing that a public recreation authority is established and that trained leadership is employed.

A monumental study, *The Roles of Public Education in Recreation,*[10] envisions six major roles for recreation:

1. Schools should educate for the worthy use of leisure.
2. Schools should achieve maximum articulation between instruction and recreation.
3. Schools should coordinate and mobilize total community resources for recreation.
4. Schools should develop cooperative planning of recreation facilities.
5. Education should encourage, stimulate, and produce research on recreation.
6. Education should stress professional preparation of recreation personnel.

MULTIPURPOSE POSSIBILITIES

School facilities, representing a larger community investment than any other tax-supported agency, are highly suitable for recreational offerings. Much school space lends itself admirably to multiple use. For example:

Auditorium (concerts, lectures, dramatics)
Gymnasium (sports, dances, play days)
Library (reading, storytelling, choral reading)

[9]H. Dan Corbin, "Education for Leisure," in Ann E. Jewett and Clyde G. Knapp (eds.), *The Growing Years: Adolescence* (Washington, D.C.: American Association of Health, Physical Education and Recreation, 1962), pp. 223–35.

[10]California State Department of Education, and California Association for Health, Physical Education and Recreation, *The Roles of Public Education in Recreation* (Sacramento, 1960).

Shop (handicrafts, appliance repairs, furniture building)

Art room (sketching, painting, sculpting)

Music or band room (choral groups, community band and orchestra, instrument and vocal instruction)

Home economics room (cooking, baking, hat making, sewing instruction)

Classrooms (clubs, language classes, quiet play)

Cafeteria (parties, dances, teas)

Swimming pool (swimming and boating instruction, splash parties, lifesaving classes)

Athletic fields (games, sports, play days)

Multipurpose room (parties, forums, get-togethers)

Laboratories (photography developing and printing, science club)

Parking lot (games, individual and dual sports, contests; after-school hours only)

SCHOOL CURRICULUM AND RECREATION

Optimum coordination should be sought between the school curriculum and recreation. While new subjects and relationships are to be encouraged, there is rich potential for recreation in the subjects now taught in the average school system. The seeds of interest, enthusiasm, and curiosity can be planted for lifelong harvesting of enriched leisure.

The school can implement curriculum–recreation coordination by setting up a special committee to determine how each subject area can best contribute to leisure education. Varied recreational opportunities for using the skills that are taught will reinforce learning. Intramural programs, club groups, pageants, festivals, exhibitions, displays, projects, and contests can further these objectives. Moreover, the recreational potentials of science, art, English, civics, and mathematics can be taught through the school camping program or the park school. In addition, the school can weld together all community recreational resources.

GOOD, BETTER, OR BEST?

Dr. Jay B. Nash, in one of his classes at New York University, stated that "the good is the worst enemy of the best." We wish to elaborate upon that statement. If, while seeking the best, you become satisfied with the good, you may make no further effort to accomplish the best. We wonder, however, what level of performance should be considered best for any particular individual: the best he is capable of, or nothing less than the absolute best that has ever been accomplished? The answer from the standpoint of education for leisure may be the best the individual can do while getting enjoyment and satisfaction from his performance. If he is striving for professional excellence, however— making a living through his particular skill or entering competition to win a championship—the absolute best should be his goal. Under such conditions, the objectives exceed those of education for leisure. But teaching the objective of the absolute best to all students, with their varying achievement levels, would be wrong, and would be missing the recreational value that can be attained by all.

SUMMARY

The school has two major responsibilities in recreation: education for leisure, and cooperation and integration of its resources with public recreation agencies. The school is our most important institution for education for leisure. Its role in providing facilities for public recreation is nearly as important.

Education for leisure is the responsibility of all teachers; however, elementary school teachers and teachers in the special fields of music, dramatics, physical education, arts, and crafts have added opportunities because of the nature of their programs, and thus have the major responsibility in contributing toward this objective. Programs must include recreational activities that can be used during leisure and, for the most part, throughout one's lifetime. Emphasis must be placed upon the participant's enjoyment and satisfaction; skill achievement should be secondary.

Suggested Reading

AMERICAN ASSOCIATION FOR HEALTH, PHYSICAL EDUCATION AND RECREATION, *Conference on Education for Leisure.* Washington, D.C., 1957.

———, *Goals for American Recreation: A Report.* Washington, D.C., 1964.

———, *Professional Preparation in Health Education, Physical Education and Recreation Education, Report of a National Conference.* Washington, D.C., 1962.

BRIGHTBILL, CHARLES K., *Man and Leisure: A Philosophy of Recreation.* Englewood Cliffs, N.J.: Prentice-Hall, Inc., 1961.

CALIFORNIA ASSOCIATION FOR HEALTH, PHYSICAL EDUCATION AND RECREATION, and State Department of Education, *The Roles of Public Education in Recreation.* Sacramento, 1957.

CORBIN, H. DAN, *Recreation Leadership.* Englewood Cliffs, N.J.: Prentice-Hall, Inc., 1970.

DANFORD, HOWARD G., *Creative Leadership in Recreation.* Boston: Allyn & Bacon, Inc., 1964.

DE GRAZIA, SEBASTIAN, *Of Time, Work and Leisure.* Garden City, N.Y.: Doubleday & Company, Inc., 1962.

HJELTE, GEORGE, and JAY S. SHIVERS, *Public Administration of Park and Recreational Services.* New York: The Macmillan Company, 1963.

JEWETT, ANN E., and CLYDE G. KNAPP, eds., *The Growing Years: Adolescence.* Washington, D.C.: American Association for Health, Physical Education and Recreation, 1962.

KRAUS, RICHARD K., *Recreation and the Schools.* New York: The Macmillan Company, 1964.

MEYER, HAROLD D., CHARLES K. BRIGHTBILL, and H. DOUGLAS SESSOMS, *Community Recreation: A Guide to Its Organization* (4th ed.). Englewood Cliffs, N.J.: Prentice-Hall, Inc., 1969.

SILBERMAN, CHARLES E., *Crisis in the Classroom.* New York: Random House, Inc., 1970.

ZEIGLER, EARLE F., *Philosophical Foundations for Physical, Health and Recreation Education.* Englewood Cliffs, N.J.: Prentice-Hall, Inc., 1968.

chapter six

PUBLIC
RECREATION

*Important as it is to organize and direct the
understanding of the world, it is more
important to organize and direct the leisure
time of the world.*

GEORGE ELIOT

Recreation is no longer simply
desirable; it is a "must," a vital essential. Authorities in the field agree
that recreation is a community responsibility. According to Harold
Meyer, Charles Brightbill, and Douglas Sessoms, "Recreation is a basic
universal desire and necessity of human life. . . . It is no less important
than welfare, health, and education to the social well-being of a people."[1]

Since recreation is common to all, it must be made a service designed
for the common welfare. It is inescapably a municipal or community-
wide responsibility to provide recreational opportunities for all ages,
races, and creeds, not only during the summer but throughout the year.
There is no single best way for all communities to meet this obligation.
However, certain basic patterns and procedures that have been ad-

[1]Harold Meyer, Charles A. Brightbill, and Douglas H. Sessoms, *Community Recreation* (Englewood Cliffs, N.J.: Prentice-Hall, Inc., 1969), pp. 163–64.

vocated by authorities and put into practice in various localities have proven successful. They are described in excellent books on specific areas in the field of recreation: the administration of recreation, leadership in recreation, recreation programs, community organization for recreation, arts and crafts in recreation, recreational music; and the like. Obviously this volume cannot deal with each topic in detail. We are concerned with the problems confronting society and the ways in which the various institutions and organizations contribute toward meeting people's recreational needs.

ADMINISTRATION

Administration is the machinery set up to carry out the functions of a particular enterprise. Administration in recreation is the organization and personnel established to conduct recreation. It must have the legal status, powers, and personnel necessary to transact its affairs and to fulfill its responsibility to society.

It would be foolhardy to prescribe one type of administrative control for all communities. There are arguments for and against each type. George Hjelte and Jay Shivers[2] present six types of administrative control with data showing the advantages and disadvantages of each.

The type of administration chosen for any particular community should be that which will render the most efficient service. It should be free of political interference and able to provide adequate funds for operation and expansion. Recreation departments must have adequate facilities and equipment for program development and enough qualified personnel to conduct the program. A high-quality administration will ensure high-quality recreation leadership. The three outstanding types of authorities responsible for providing community park and recreation services were traditionally recreation, park, and school departments; however, the recent trend has been to combine recreation and park departments into a single government agency responsible for public recreation.

There is no question about the necessity for cooperative effort among the park department, the schools, and the public recreation department. Cooperation is usually voluntary, as it is exceedingly difficult to legislate cooperative effort. Combining the park and public recreation departments makes coordinated effort more likely, especially if the

[2]George Hjelte and Jay S. Shivers, *Public Administration of Park and Recreational Services* (New York: The Macmillan Company, 1963), pp. 57–70.

responsibility of the combined department is clearly defined and the administrator is qualified by training and experience to direct such a department. When the recreation department is placed under an established park department in the role of "stepchild," an unhealthy condition exists.

LEGAL ASPECTS OF RECREATION ORGANIZATION

Legal authority through state legislation is necessary for the organization of a public recreation department. The states have been granted considerable authority, subject only to the powers reserved to the federal government under the United States Constitution. The states are permitted to provide for local government by granting charters which give the cities certain powers and establish their corporate existence. According to Hjelte and Shivers,

> Home rule consists essentially in the power to make and amend the municipal charter. Several states have provided for home rule in more or less complete fashion. In other states the powers of cities are exercised under state statutes universally applicable to all cities of specified classes other than cities exercising the right to adopt individual charters. The right of any city to organize, promote, conduct, and otherwise provide for recreational service rests upon the powers granted to the city by the general state laws or the city charter or through the general provisions of home rule.[3]

In organizing local public recreation departments it is necessary to make sure that the charter grants the municipality sufficient legislative power; charter amendment may be needed to grant such powers. Wording must be specific. Enabling acts should authorize the local government to establish a particular agency with power to provide revenues either by appropriation or by taxation and to carry out its responsibilities. The power to acquire property such as land or buildings, whether owned by the municipality and readily available or through private purchase, condemnation, or gift, should be included. The grant must also include the authority to construct and maintain buildings, playgrounds, swimming pools, and athletic fields and to acquire the equipment and personnel necessary to promote and conduct recreation programs for the health, welfare, and enjoyment of the people.

[3] *Ibid.,* p. 15.

COMMUNITY ORGANIZATION FOR
RECREATION

Community organization for recreation should also include the
coordination of the efforts of the various institutions and organizations
in the community toward fulfilling the recreational needs of the people.
A communitywide organization for recreation is necessary for the sake
of economy in finances and effort. Cooperative effort avoids duplication
among the various agencies and organizations involved in recreational
programming.

Integrating the efforts among the public-supported departments of
parks, recreation, and schools can save many dollars. In a number of
cities the park department is responsible for the construction and maintenance of recreation facilities such as gymnasiums, swimming pools,
athletic fields, tennis courts, and golf courses. Schools use these facilities
to teach skills and to develop attitudes and appreciation through their
physical education and recreation education programs, while public
recreation departments use the facilities to provide the public with
recreation programs and leadership. Further cooperative effort with
federal and state recreation departments would be effective and highly
desirable.

FINANCE

The financial support for a recreation program is directly pro-
portional to its interpreted value to the public. Our value systems are
greatly influenced, even controlled, by communication. Too often we
emphasize, without clarifying its basic value, an immediate specific
activity that withers and dies as many fads do. Financial support must
be based on a definite policy which is in turn based on a sound philosophy. For example, the policy that the municipality will furnish the
facility and basic leadership, with all other expenses borne by the participants, is based on the philosophy that urban man is reticent about
communicating and sharing with his neighbors.[4] It is therefore the duty
of the governing body to satisfy by some means the basic need of man

---

[4]See David Riesman, et al., *The Lonely Crowd: A Study of the Changing American
Character* (rev. ed.) (New Haven, Conn.: Yale University Press, 1950), for an eloquent
portrayal of this phenomenon.

to be a member of a group. The municipality may choose to do this through the establishment of a recreation department.

While expenditures for parks and recreation vary from community to community, eight to ten dollars per person can provide adequate recreation programs and leadership, providing existing facilities are used. The amount of money necessary for capital improvements will depend on what facilities the community has and the requirements of an adequate program. Capital improvements such as construction of recreation centers, auditoriums, stadiums, and athletic fields must come from funds provided for that purpose.

Recreation has usually been financed through appropriations from the general tax fund or a specific recreation tax. The capital improvement budget is variably raised through either appropriation or bond issue. Many departments have been forced to use part of their operational budget to expand and acquire additional facilities. This means a sacrifice in program and leadership, the prime functions of the department. The solution to the problem of finance is the promotion and conduct of public recreation in such a way that people are made to realize the vital significance of the program.

Financial Earnings

Recreation departments have been forced to charge fees for certain services or privileges because of the inadequate funds provided by appropriation or special tax. This has been justified on the grounds that certain activities are enjoyed by only a small proportion of the taxpayers, and that those who benefit from the program should pay proportionately. The practice of charging a small green fee for the privilege of playing golf and a towel or locker fee at swimming pools is now accepted as standard procedure.

The recreation administration must remember, however, that it is rendering a public service and is supported by public tax funds. Turning the operation of a municipal golf course over to a commercial enterprise, or charging exorbitant green fees, is contrary to every principle of public recreation.

How do recreation departments handle these "extra" services? Lynn Rodney categorizes the services for which fees are charged as follows:[5]

[5]Lynn S. Rodney, *Administration of Public Recreation* (New York: The Ronald Press Company, 1964), p. 281.

1. Special features and facilities, including use of golf courses, swimming pools, boating facilities, bath houses, tennis courts, picnic accommodations, game areas, bowling greens
2. Exclusive occupancy (rental), including exclusive use by individuals or groups of clubrooms, auditoriums, gymnasiums, swimming pools, stadia, and the like
3. Rental of specialized equipment, including rental or service charge for use of costumes, athletic equipment, radios or phonographs, projectors and screens, kitchen and banquet equipment, boats, horses, and the like
4. Materials and supplies, including those items that are used and consumed in special activities such as drama, music, handicrafts, social activities, and the like
5. Special instructors, including only those giving highly specialized instruction that does not fall within the general services of the program staff
6. Special accommodations, including such accommodations and items of a special nature as parking for special occasions, fuel for heating, special meetings, and special services

The practice of granting concessions to private operators is questionable. Some people advocate the practice on the grounds that a public agency should not enter into competition with private business. However, most experienced administrators feel that the public recreation department has a responsibility to provide the comforts and conveniences associated with its programs. Taxpayers' money provides the golf course; no private enterprise should profit from the public's investment.

Recreation facilities and programs are provided for the benefit of the people; the degree to which this objective is reached depends on the number of people who benefit from the program. Comforts and conveniences necessary for its successful operation are a responsibility of the recreation department. These conveniences should not be primarily for profit, but rather to serve the people. Any profit gained and retained by the department is returned to the taxpayer in the form of additional and improved services.

The practice of granting concessions creates a climate that encourages the use of political influence for private gain. In many instances, concessionaires employ in their operations commercial practices that do not uphold high standards, especially when standards conflict with profits.

Another source of revenue is admissions to athletic contests. This varies with the size of the community, the seating capacity of the facility, the type of event, and the public interest.

FACILITIES

The problem of providing facilities for use in the public recreation program varies in different locations. In some cases recreation departments own their facilities and may have limited or no arrangements for the use of school or park department buildings or grounds. In other localities recreation departments have no facilities of their own and must depend on facilities owned by the school or park departments. Still other recreation departments have facilities of their own and in addition, use those controlled by the school or park departments. Sufficient facilities are necessary for an adequate program. The public recreation department should be able to use all facilities of the park and school departments.

The school and park departments should assume the responsibility of coordinating their facilities with the public recreation department. The park department should refrain from operating recreation programs; that is the function of the recreation department. Combining the park and recreation departments under one qualified administrator solves the problem of cooperative effort.

The use of school grounds for public recreation has not been entirely satisfactory, even when cooperation between the two agencies has been established. A particular type of landscape architecture is essential for a well-designed playground. Schoolgrounds are rarely so well-designed. We might question the importance of constructing schoolgrounds in accordance with playground standards, but it is obvious that a well-designed playground is attractive and serviceable to both school and public recreation programs. The cost of such schoolgrounds is a great deal less than that of two such areas. The central location of the school meets the needs for recreation. New York City has been tremendously successful in planning and operating joint school and park department playgrounds. Having a qualified landscape architect design the schoolgrounds in accordance with playground standards results in considerable savings of dollars.

Play Lot

The play lot has been recommended for the use of preschool children. It is most important in congested inner-city areas where children are deprived of backyard play space. It should be approximately twenty-five hundred square feet in area with a service radius of one-fourth mile.

It may be a separate facility or part of a larger playground. The area should be fenced for protection of the children and landscaped for beautification as well as for shade. It should include the usual play apparatus, such as slides, swings, teeter-totters, and sand box. Manufacturers are now providing such equipment in novel and attractive designs that encourage creative play.

The Neighborhood Playground

The standards for measuring the quality of neighborhood playgrounds include acreage, beautification, provisions for particular activities, and safety. The neighborhood playground is the chief outdoor play facility for children of elementary school age. Effort has been made to include in the playground program activities of interest for the whole family. Such programs have been so successful the past few years that it is now recommended that the neighborhood playground include facilities for all family members.

The area should be approximately five acres, depending on the population it is to serve. Allowance should be made for 150 square feet per child playing at one time. The design of this playground is vitally important to its ability to render maximum service. It should be attractive, a fact which is seldom appreciated by community officials. Beautification attracts children to the playground; program and leadership will keep them coming. Some people advocate that as much as one-third of the total area should be allocated to beautification. Trees are essential, giving both beauty and shade. Areas should be laid out for particular uses. The play lot for the school child and the area for such games as basketball, volleyball, badminton, paddle tennis, and regulation tennis call for all-weather surfaces. Other activities such as shuffleboard and roller skating also require hard-surface areas. Activities such as softball, archery, and soccer require turf. The area for dramatics and music should include a stage, with shrubbery to facilitate entrance and exit of actors and performers. Fencing of the entire area should also incorporate shrubbery, to subdue noise and to beautify.

The Playfield

The playfield is a recreation area that often includes both indoor and outdoor facilities for all ages. It can be connected with a high school building or a community recreation center. In some localities it is combined with a city park, providing an ideal recreational service.

The playfield area may vary from ten to twenty acres, depending on the population to be served. If the field is connected with a high school, twenty acres is recommended. In small communities whose high schools have small enrollments, a minimum of ten acres may serve the needs of the students.

The Recreation and Park Area

A recreation and park area should provide for the recreation activities of the community and enhance the scenic beauty of the outdoors. It can be fifty acres or more in size, depending on the local situation. Some parks contain thousands of acres.

Specialized Areas and Facilities

Many recreation activities require particular facilities. These facilities should be provided if the recreation program is to meet the varied needs of all in the community.

The Golf Course. The number of golf courses needed depends on the population within the service area. Many communities handicapped by lack of space have been limited to nine-hole golf courses. An eighteen-hole course will accommodate three times as many players as a nine-hole course because of the area over which they are distributed. A clubhouse, putting green, and parking area are essential; they should be near the first and tenth tees and the ninth and eighteenth greens.

Swimming Facilities. Swimming and wading pools are essential even if bathing beaches are available. Much of the recreation program depends upon the pool facility. The bathhouse should adjoin adequate space for tables and attractive shade umbrellas, which will be thoroughly appreciated by pool users.

Auditorium. The municipal auditorium is becoming essential in cities throughout America. They range from simple one-service buildings with only an auditorium to huge structures including a coliseum, large and small theaters, courts, swimming pools, meeting rooms, and so on, for example, the Municipal Auditorium of Kansas City, Missouri. It seems economical to include all the needed facilities under one roof. The population and needs of the community should be factors in determining what is included in the structure. In certain communities a very large theater is essential; in others, a large theater would be entirely unsuitable.

Because of the increasing popularity of basketball tournaments, a large city can at least partially fund a coliseum of huge seating capacity through rentals or admissions. People like to see skilled performances. Consider, for example, the colleges and universities that have become powers in the collegiate basketball world; many have recently built huge basketball arenas or coliseums.

The Stadium. It is much easier to arouse support for the construction of a stadium than for an auditorium. Interest in sports is high, as we can see from the length of the newspaper sports section. When a staff of sports writers "beats the drums" for a municipal stadium, they are generally successful.

For many communities the stadium is a highly desirable facility. Many a large city has found it a profit-making contributor to the municipal recreation budget. A stadium also provides an opportunity for a more expanded and varied program of recreation. It may include a mobile or fixed stage so that large audiences can listen to concerts and musicals. This increases its utility beyond the customary events—football, baseball, and track and field.

The Recreation Building. The recreation building and its facilities should be determined by community needs. If adequate gymnasiums are provided through cooperation with schools, a gymnasium in the recreation center may be a less pressing need, though still desirable. Gymnasiums with locker rooms and showers are essential to a sound recreation program. The building should include facilities for a well-rounded program. A dramatics program, for example, would necessitate an auditorium (its size determined by the population served), dressing rooms, toilets, and a room for making and storing the wardrobe. Craft rooms with storage space for supplies should be included in the building, along with rooms for painting and sketching. Music rooms for band or orchestra practice, as well as smaller rooms for individual instrumental and vocal rehearsing are also needed.

Programs to meet the needs of groups with special interests, such as dance, handicrafts, or photography, are a vital part of a public recreation plan. Facilities for group meetings and programs are essential, as are a check room, lounge, game room, and adequate office space for staff.

Land adjacent to the building is highly desirable to provide for the outdoor program that should be included in the service of the recreation center to the community. This space can be used for parking at concerts or other special events. In colder climates it can be flooded for use as an ice rink. A swimming pool is a valuable addition, with the climate determining whether it shall be indoors, outdoors, or even the outdoor–indoor type.

PROGRAM

As we become more affluent and discerning, we grow more sensitive to our basic needs. The conditions of modern society pose grave problems, among them the expanding need to cope with uncommitted time. Recreation, more than any other single force, has the potential to educate us for more meaningful leisure.

A wide range of activities are necessary to meet the needs and interests of people with varied backgrounds, experiences, and levels of "recreational literacy." Some find success, satisfaction, and profit from a particular type of activity while others will not. Some satisfy their needs through an athletic program, some through crafts and art, others through music, or dramatics, depending upon the particular liking, talents, and needs of each. Recreation programs must be arranged and conducted to meet the needs and interests of all.

The area of recreation is as broad as human interest. For simpler analysis it can be divided into the following categories:

Aquatic activities
Arts and crafts
Boating, canoeing, and sailing
Club organizations
Dance
Dramatics and story telling
Hobbies
Individual and dual sports
Leadership principles
Leadership techniques
Low and high organized games
Music
Outdoor education and camping
Social recreation
Special events
Team sports

Embarking on the Program

The special interest program includes a wide variety of activities such as photography, stamp collecting, and garden clubs. Special interest programs are primarily self-directed, requiring little time from the administrator. His efforts generally involve instigation of particular programs, assistance in organization, and provision of space for meetings and guidance. The special interest program can and should contribute widely to the community. It can reach all ages and stimulate a wide variety of beneficial leisure-time activities.

In the beginning, the recreation program was conceived of and conducted purely as a summer playground program, inaugurated to meet the needs of the underprivileged child and consisting of sports and games. Cultural and creative activities were so rare that they were later referred to as "the neglected areas of recreation."

The recreation program and facilities should provide the opportunity for people to satisfy their needs. The breadth of the program determines the extent of the individual's opportunity and possible satisfactions. But facilities and program will not ensure the desired results; the quality of leadership is also a prime factor.

LEADERSHIP

The fact that leadership is most significant in determining whether benefits are derived through recreation is little appreciated by most people. The prevailing opinion is that practically anyone is qualified to direct a recreation program. This attitude has not encouraged quality recreation programming.

Leadership is responsible for progress, and will be a determining factor in the future. Human resources, especially of children, are of inestimable importance. We spend great sums of public money to improve the breeds of hogs, cattle, and crops. We spend a terrifying amount of money to maintain our penal institutions. The cost of welfare payments mounts every year. Yet the taxpayer appears unwilling to spend an adequate amount to provide for skilled leadership for his children.

Leadership determines the success or failure of any program. A good leader can bring rich rewards from a meager program; a poor leader can ruin the best program ever conceived. Remember that an activity is neither good nor bad in itself. Its effect on the individual determines whether it is good or bad for him, and leadership determines that effect. The standards of conduct set, the ideals established, and the goals and rewards sought are of vital significance. The leader must direct the situation to bring about the desired returns. Leadership can be soundly executed through different forms of control.

The leader must understand his charges. He must be able to "speak their language"; if he cannot, no rapport will be established. He must recognize their problems and needs. Through his efforts, they can be helped and guided along the paths of normal thought and behavior.

Securing Qualified Leadership

Several vital problems are involved in meeting community needs for qualified leaders in recreation. The problems seem to lead in a vicious circle.

1. There are too few professionally qualified leaders in the immediate community.
2. Because of the lack of qualified people, partially qualified personnel must be employed.
3. If the partially qualified people are locals, a precedent is established that primarily local people will be hired.
4. Because the people are only partially qualified, they will have to accept low pay, and a low salary scale will be established.
5. The low salary scale will discourage potentially qualified people from preparing themselves professionally for recreation leadership.

How can a community expect to have professionally qualified recreation personnel if the salary scale is lower than the prevailing wage for school teachers? The public should be made more aware of the importance of professionally trained and qualified leadership. We must be willing to provide sufficient funds to pay recreation leaders at least the prevailing wage for school teachers.[6] We must be willing to employ professionally prepared and qualified leaders from the available sources, wherever they may be. Finally, we should mandate the establishment of a government agency to set standards of certification for recreation leaders similar to the standards set by state departments of

[6]The National Recreation and Parks Association will not recommend a candidate for a position paying less than $7,200 a year.

education for the certification of school teachers. These suggestions for raising the standards for recreation leadership are hardly revolutionary. They have already been achieved in education. After all, recreation is acknowledged by educators to be "the worthy use of leisure." Hence, the importance of recreation cannot be overemphasized. Recreation should occupy as important a place in our social structure as education.

PUBLIC RELATIONS

Publications and publicity are often considered interchangeable. However, public relations is more than publicity. Publicity means providing information; public relations means interpretation and recognition. Recreation departments must be concerned with adequate and desirable publicity to make the public aware of what is going on, when, and where. All available media should be used for providing information to the public. The press and radio and television announcements are familiar to us all, but certain other procedures may be overlooked. Volunteer leaders and committees contributing their time and effort provide excellent means for publicizing the work of the department. They are valuable parts of public relations. The recreation department's staff has a highly vital role. They are sold on the value of their work and proud of their part in its success. They are the chief ambassadors of goodwill; the department is judged by their teamwork and by the effectiveness with which its policies are relayed to participants in all recreation areas.

There is probably no other branch of community service to which the goodwill of the community is so important as to public recreation. The recreation program must meet the needs and interests of the community. Their ideas and opinions are important. Many community members know how they want to use their leisure time, but do not have the opportunity; the public recreation department can provide that opportunity. More fortunate members of society, who can arrange for their recreational activities are of no direct concern to the recreation department, with the possible exception that they may accept an invitation to serve as volunteer leaders or club advisers to hobby groups and the like.

The recreation department should survey the community to determine people's interests and needs. Public acknowledgement of the recreation department's efforts is a step toward good public relations.

Public relations for a recreation department should be in the hands of a qualified person. The public relations director, like the leader should have a great deal of native ability. His personality, appearance, judgment, and tact are important. In addition, he should be qualified and trained for the work. Humility is a virtue that reaps valuable returns; the opinionated and arrogant individual will find the going rough and unproductive.

MAINTENANCE

Satisfactory maintenance of facilities presents a problem for the administrator of the public recreation department. If the recreation department is independent of the park department and controls its own facilities, then it must provide maintenance, of necessity duplicating the equipment and personnel of the park department. Such a situation is wasteful of money and effort; a practical solution would be for the park department to assume the responsibility of maintenance for the recreation department. If, on the other hand, the recreation and park department are consolidated, a central maintenance division handles the work for both, at a considerable saving.

The suggestion that the park department construct and maintain all recreation facilities for the community, including those to be used by the recreation department, the public schools, and the park facilities merits serious consideration. The cost of duplicating maintenance equipment, personnel, and facilities is prohibitive. The park department should limit its efforts to construction and maintenance. The public schools teach skills and develop attitudes and appreciations of recreational activities, using the facilities provided by the park department. The recreation department uses all the facilities and furnishes leadership for the entire community. With such an arrangement, all the agencies would fulfill their functions without overlapping of efforts or expense. Many communities are adopting a consolidated plan with marked success.

PLANNING

An examination of the growth of recreation in the United States reveals vast sums of money misspent because of a lack of long-range planning. As public recreation is relatively new, it is not surprising to find inadequate provisions for recreation in many older cities. Where an attempt has been made to meet people's needs, it has often been done at an exorbitant cost. Long-range planning is necessary to meet future needs at minimum cost. Qualified planners can project population trends and aid recreation programming, determining the areas and facilities that will be needed. With this information, the necessary property can be secured and made available before the need becomes critical. Preparing the public for the expansion necessary to meet future needs requires concerted effort. Obtaining the taxpayer support necessary to float a bond issue calls for a great deal of promotion.

Planning, then, necessitates not only a long-range view of the needs of the people, but also a long-range view of the procedures necessary to carry out the program. People must become aware of the importance of recreation and accept as their responsibility the provision of recreational opportunities for all. Until this has been accomplished communities will be handicapped in the development of adequate recreation facilities, programs, and leadership.

RECORDS AND REPORTS

The recreation department is accountable to the public for the expenditure of tax funds. A complete record of all finances must be kept. The department must show where the money comes from—taxes, appropriations, and earnings—and how the money is expended. Books must be audited and reports filed. The public must be kept informed in regard to the finances of the department.

Financial reports must be made from time to time. An annual report should be prepared not only for the board of commissions, but also for the administrator in preparing his budget for the ensuing year. The annual report is also valuable in the department's long-range planning. Records of income and cost of operation are indicative of future needs as the department grows and expands its services to the community.

RURAL RECREATION

The organization of rural recreation varies in different localities. The increase in numbers and programs of county recreation departments in certain sections of the country nas been outstanding. The recreation program of the Union County Park System of Union County, New Jersey is an example. Westchester County, New York and St. Louis County, Minnesota are further examples of counties with extensive programs in recreation.

Recreational opportunities must be available to people of all ages the year around. That education for leisure is essential to prepare people to take part in recreational opportunities has already been established. The success of a rural recreation program depends on the cooperation of all the agencies in the community: school, church, government agencies, agricultural extension service, and civic and youth service organizations. The federal Cooperative Agricultural Extension Service contributes significantly to the recreational lives of those living in rural areas. Among its recreational offerings are arts, crafts, music, recreation leadership, tourism, and photography. The unified efforts of all agencies are necessary. The greatest problem of rural recreation is organization; however, problems of isolation, transportation, leadership, and finance can be met through consolidated effort.

SUMMARY

Public recreation is a community responsibility. It occupies as important a place in our society as education. It must be paid for from tax funds, either by appropriation or by means of a special recreational tax. It must be incorporated in the city charter or in an ordinance adopted by the municipal legislative body.

The responsiblity for providing recreational programs and leadership for the entire community is primarily a local one. The recreation department must provide facilities or have the use of facilities provided by other government organizations in the community. A successful department must be internally organized so that its program and services can be efficiently handled by a competent staff using adequate facilities.

The areas of responsibility of a municipal recreation department include the following:

1. Administration provides the machinery through which the department operates.
2. The administration must plan to meet the needs of the future efficiently and economically.

3. Finances should be planned to enable the department to handle its fiscal needs.
4. The department should have the use of facilities needed to conduct its program.
5. The program should offer activities aimed at reaching the desired goals.
6. Leadership must be competent to achieve the goals.
7. Sound public relations should establish goodwill and develop an informed citizenry.
8. Facilities should be maintained at a high level to foster pride in the physical layout.
9. Records and reports are necessary for efficient operation, to account for the expenditure of public funds, and to keep the public informed.
10. Recreation for the rural dweller constitutes a fundamental concern. The Cooperative Agricultural Extension Service, through its 4-H Youth Development Program contributes effectively.

Suggested Reading

AMERICAN ASSOCIATION FOR HEALTH, PHYSICAL EDUCATION AND RECREATION, *Goals for American Recreation: A Report.* Washington, D.C.: American Association for Health, Physical Education and Recreation, 1964.

BUTLER, GEORGE B., *Introduction to Community Recreation,* 4th ed. (prepared for the National Recreation Association). New York: McGraw-Hill Book Company, 1967.

CARLSON, REYNOLD, THEODORE DEPPE, and JANET MACLEAN, *Recreation in American Life.* Belmont, Calif.: Wadsworth Publishing Company, Inc., 1963.

CORBIN, H. DAN, *Recreation Leadership,* 3rd ed. Englewood Cliffs, N.J.: Prentice-Hall, Inc., 1970.

DE GRAZIA, SEBASTIAN, *Of Time, Work and Leisure.* Garden City, N.Y.: Doubleday & Company, Inc., 1962.

HJELTE, GEORGE, and JAY S. SHIVERS, *Public Administration of Park and Recreational Services.* New York: The Macmillan Company, 1963.

HOFFER, ERIC, *The Temper of Our Time.* New York: Harper & Row, Publishers, 1967.

KRAUS, RICHARD G., *Recreation and the Schools.* New York: The Macmillan Company, 1966.

MEYER, HAROLD D., CHARLES K. BRIGHTBILL, and H. DOUGLAS SESSOMS, *Community Recreation.* Englewood Cliffs, N.J.: Prentice-Hall, Inc., 1969.

OUTDOOR RECREATION RESOURCES REVIEW COMMISSION, *Outdoor Recreation for America.* Washington, D.C.: Outdoor Recreation Resources Review Commission, 1962.

RODNEY, LYNN S., *Administration of Public Recreation.* New York: The Ronald Press Company, 1964.

SHIRLEY, MAX, and HOWARD G. DANFORD, *Creative Leadership in Recreation,* 2nd ed. Boston: Allyn & Bacon, Inc., 1970.

TOYNBEE, ARNOLD J., *Change and Habit: The Challenge of Our Time.* New York: Oxford University Press, 1966.

"ASIDE FROM NOT LISTING *CULTURAL LEISURE*,
THEY FAIL TO MENTION A *CURLING CLUB*."

chapter seven

INDUSTRIAL
RECREATION

*To be able to fill leisure intelligently is the
last product of civilization.*

BERTRAND RUSSELL

BACKGROUND HIGHLIGHTS

Since the beginning of recorded history individuals have been
interested in the welfare of mankind. At times, these individuals would
band together in efforts to improve conditions that were detrimental
to the health and welfare. Generally, they met with little success. Only
after years of effort and gradual growth in number did their influence
produce results, and even then, it was often the result of tragedy. For
example, the Iriquois Theater fire in Chicago provided the impetus for
legislation regarding safe construction of structures used by the public.

People have also been concerned with the welfare of workers in
factories where health and safety conditions were deplorable. Pleas on
the grounds of human welfare accomplished little, but when the approach was made on the basis of increased financial returns for the

employer, things began to change. Every day a worker was absent from his job because of sickness or injury, the company's productivity decreased. The new significance of the worker changed the employer's attitude. Guard devices were installed on machinery to prevent accidents, and lighting and ventilation were improved. Modern factories are carefully designed to protect the health and safety of the employees.

The realization that happy, contented employees make industry more economical spurred the development of industrial recreation. Management has attempted to improve not only the working conditions but also the living conditions of employees, by means of industrial housing, shopping centers, and recently the development of parks and recreation. Before deciding on a plant site, enlightened employers consider the availability of adequate recreational areas and schools as vital factors.

FACTORS TO CONSIDER

Industries located in large cities where real estate companies and city management have anticipated population growth encounter relatively few housing problems. Other industrial concerns are somewhat isolated, with plant personnel constituting all or practically all of the population of the community. In such situations management must often ensure suitable living conditions to secure and retain employees. An adequate recreation program must be provided either by management or by management and labor.

In some cities active and efficient public recreation departments meet the needs of the industrial workers. In other communities, the public recreation department, other organizations interested in the leisure-time activities of the people, and industrial management all coordinate their efforts to meet the entire community's needs.

TYPES OF ADMINISTRATIVE PATTERNS

Industrial recreation programs are administered and financed in many different ways. The following are some variations now in operation:

1. The program may be administered entirely by management. In this case, the physical plant, including land, facilities, and equipment, is provided by the company. Company-employed recreation leaders operate the program, offered at little or no cost to the worker.
2. Management may provide land, facilities, and equipment for a program operated cooperatively by management and labor.
3. Management may provide the land, facilities, and equipment for an employee-operated program.
4. Employees may finance and operate the program entirely by themselves. In this case, management gives some consideration. Employees may be given concession rights to enable them to raise money to finance the program. Work schedules may be arranged to allow time for attention to program administration.

In many communities the YMCA and similar organizations work through their membership to conduct recreational activities for industrial workers. All types of industrial recreation programs are in operation throughout the United States. Industry is aware of the mutual advantage of involving the worker and his family in recreational activities.

Finance

Financial arrangements vary in accordance with industry administrative policy toward recreation. Funds can be raised through the sale of soft drinks, candy, and cigarettes; the operation of cafeterias and canteens; and the sale of athletic and recreation equipment.

A recreation association may be established for employees and their families, with membership dues providing at least a portion of the funds for recreation. For certain activities, admission may be charged to defray operating cost and even realize a profit.

The trend seems to be toward a combination of all of the methods we have discussed. Customarily the company provides facilities and a qualified director. Large industrial establishments provide additional trained personnel to assure a diversified program that is efficiently conducted. Volunteer leaders can work in industrial recreation just as in public recreation. Regardless of how the program is financed, professionally qualified leadership is essential.

PROGRAM

The industrial recreation program, like any public recreation program, should be directed at meeting the needs and interests of all: not only the employees, but their families and retired employees as well. The program should take the participant into account but not overlook the spectator. At times we desire the relaxation, enjoyment, and satisfaction of spectating, for example, listening to a musical concert.

While athletics and sports of all types are most popular, music, dramatics and social activities are also an important part of a well-conceived program. Outings, camping, hunting, trap and skeet shooting, and fishing are popular individual and family activities. Square dancing has increased in popularity throughout the United States during the past decade.

An industrial recreation program is economical to both management and labor. A wholesome, varied, and interesting program with proper guidance and leadership will satisfy the individual's needs and contribute to his health and efficiency. It will also contribute toward a cooperative relationship between the employees and management.

SCHEDULE OF EVENTS

The recreation program schedule must suit the leisure time of those for whom activities are arranged. Some plants operate on a twenty-four-hour basis, involving three personnel shifts. While employees may work a particular shift only for two weeks or so, their leisure needs must be considered even for that short period of time. The shift from 11 PM to 7 AM is referred to as the "dogshift," or "graveyard shift." Dogshift workers may enjoy an early-evening recreation program. However, the workers who begin at 3 PM and work until 11 PM would be left out of early-evening recreation.

The lunch hour is a highly suitable time for a rich recreation program. The worker who eats his lunch and sits out the rest of his lunch hour has little break from the monotony of his job. A short but interesting recreation period would refresh him for the afternoon. If meals are served in dining rooms or cafeterias, the recreation program will tend to reduce congestion in these facilities as workers move to the recreation areas. The meal break is one of the most fruitful, readily arranged, and convenient recreation periods for employee and employer alike.

Innumerable activities are suitable for the lunch hour program. Common activities include table tennis, volleyball, horseshoes, bowling, checkers, dominoes, chess, billiards, pool, shuffleboard, sketching, craft projects, card games, music, movies, short dramatic skits, and variety shows. Opportunities should be provided for special interest groups to meet. A library, reading room, and record listening room should also be available.

While it is probably considered more valuable to be a participant, great enjoyment is also available for the spectator. Competitive activities that develop rivalry between branches or departments within the company engage the lively interest of the spectators and followers of their respective teams.

INDUSTRIAL CAMPS

Camp programs for employees and their families are growing in popularity; a campsite and minimal facilities are generally provided by the company. The program is usually informal, carried on by the employees under the guidance of the recreation staff. The camp may be available for family use on a reservation basis. Fees may be charged for particular services. Schedules may be arranged for specific groups or special-interest groups. The camp will be valuable for weekend use and in some instances for employee vacations.

The site of the camp and the activities available contribute to its popularity. Many activities are seasonal; for example, a well-stocked lake or stream will invariably attract fishermen. Hunting seasons are set by law; some other activities are influenced by climate. Recreation directors should be aware of seasonal activities, and schedule accordingly.

Industrial recreation programs have expanded so much that national tournaments are now held in team and individual events like golf, bowling, softball, basketball, and trap and skeet shooting.

A program of self-directed activities constitutes the major part of the recreation program in some industrial plants. A professionally qualified director is charged with the administration of the program. A recreation association elects officers and appoints standing committees, each with a particular function. The various committees, organized around special interests, conduct the programs.

LEADERSHIP

Industrial recreation administration includes both professionally qualified and volunteer leaders. Both are essential in achieving program goals.

The number of professionally trained personnel needed to conduct the program should be determined by the size of the industrial concern: the number of employees, the number and range of facilities, and the location of the industry in regard to the total community. Many a large industry in a big city has developed a fine industrial recreation program with only one professionally qualified director and possibly a trained assistant. The use of volunteer employees with particular interests and abilities has made this practice successful. However, there is no substitute for qualified leadership. Since recreation is a joyous, wholesome experience engaged in by choice, with no reward other than personal satisfactions, it should be directed by capable and understanding leadership.

COOPERATION BETWEEN INDUSTRY AND
COMMUNITY

In communities where public recreation has been developed and organized satisfactorily, industrial recreation programs should be coordinated with public programs. Cooperation of industrial officials with those in the municipality will be necessary. The provision of recreation facilities by industrial management for employees will still bring valuable returns; pride of possession and identity with a parent organization are human nature, and conducive to stability within the group.

A classical example is that of the Oakland, California Recreation Department and the Industrial Athletic Association of Metropolitan Oakland. Leadership and equipment are provided by the city for organizing and conducting intramural tournaments as well as interplant competition. This citywide organization has grown considerably since its inception in 1919. In 1940 the IAA was incorporated. The pattern of Oakland's organization for industry has been followed by many cities throughout the United States.

The core of the IAA program is interplant competition. In addition to softball, basketball, golf, and bowling, the IAA organizes competition in tennis, table tennis, touch football, swimming, horseback riding, crew, and folk dancing. The Recreation Department provides able assistance through assigned supervisors. All IAA activities and facility use are coordinated with the Recreation Department's regular adult program.

Community recreation organization should encompass not only facilities but also programs to interest the entire community. Therefore, organization within industry becomes part of the overall plan. Coordinating committees within plants should establish and maintain liaison between the community and the industrial recreation program. Jackson Anderson elaborates:

> The recreation activities and facilities provided by the local community will greatly influence the selection of activities for the company program. A significant trend is seen in the fact that industries are making an effort to coordinate their employee recreation programs with the recreation programs provided by the local municipality, the YMCA and the YWCA and other community agencies. Companies are finding that through coordinating their programs with the local community program, they are making available to their employees a greater offering of recreation activities. ... Through such coordination needless duplication of activities may be avoided.[1]

SAMPLE INDUSTRIAL SETUPS

For those who are interested in a more detailed study of particular types of industrial recreation, we name here a few industries that represent the different situations we have mentioned in this chapter. The Hershey Chocolate Company in Hershey, Pennsylvania is located in a community that exists because of the company. Hershey Chocolate has taken notable care of its employees. The recreation areas, facilities, and program are designed to meet the needs of the employees and their families. Another good recreation program provided by an industrial

---

[1]Jackson M. Anderson, *Industrial Recreation* (New York: McGraw-Hill Book Company, 1955), p. 100.

concern in an isolated situation is that of the West Point Manufacturing Company. The company has five small company towns and provides a program for the people in each of these locations. Examples of good employee recreation programs in medium-size cities are those of the United States Steel Corporation of Gary, Indiana and the General Electric Company in Schenectady, New York. Large companies that sponsor excellent employee recreation programs in metropolitan industrial cities are the General Motors Corporation (Detroit, Michigan) and the Goodyear Rubber Company (Akron, Ohio), which provide services for thousands of employees and their families.

SUMMARY

Many industries in the United States are contributing to the satisfaction of human needs through their recreation programs. Industrial recreation programs are on the increase; through the cooperation of management and labor, many people are benefitting from the wholesome use of their leisure. Recreation programs are run in situations from the isolated industry which forms the little community to the industries in our metropolises.

The type of administration and finance is generally determined by management and labor. In small communities, management may shoulder a greater share of the cost of activities. In larger communities, more equitable sharing between management and labor is common.

We must recognize the importance of preparing to use leisure wisely. There must be a concerted effort on the part of the municipality, industry, and the citizenry. The public must be well informed about the recreational opportunities provided by the various institutions and organizations.

Selected Reading

ANDERSON, JACKSON M., Industrial Recreation. New York: McGraw-Hill Book Company, 1955.

CORBIN, H. DAN, Recreation Leadership (3rd ed.). Englewood Cliffs, N.J.: Prentice-hall, Inc., 1970.

DIEHL, L. J., and FLOYD R. EASTWOOD, *Industrial Recreation, Its Development and Present Status.* Lafayette, Ind.: Purdue University, 1940.

MEYER, HAROLD D., CHARLES K. BRIGHTBILL, and H. DOUGLAS SESSOMS, *Community Recreation: A Guide to Its Organization.* Englewood Cliffs, N.J.: Prentice-Hall, Inc., 1970.

ROMNEY, G. OTT, *Off the Job Living.* New York: A. S. Barnes & Co., Inc., 1946.

chapter eight

RECREATION
AND
REHABILITATION

The greatest personal defeat of man is the
difference between what he is capable of
becoming and what he, in fact, became.

ASHLEY MONTAGU

If we accept the thesis that recreation can contribute toward the satisfaction of basic human needs, we must also recognize that it has a place in the rehabilitation and/or habilitation of individuals suffering from some form of abnormality. All of us, regardless of disability, need recreational pursuits. Individual differences in need are but a matter of kind and degree. Those who need rehabilitation are functioning under limiting physical, emotional, neurological, or social conditions, or a combination of these factors.

LEADERSHIP CONSIDERATIONS

Leadership is of vital importance in achieving goals through recreation. Leadership for rehabilitation is not appreciably different from other recreation leadership, except that such leaders must understand the needs and limitations of their charges. Their professional preparation must include technical terminology and practices in keeping with medical and psychiatric recommendations. (It is noteworthy that all psychiatrists are physicians, but not all physicians are psychiatrists.)

Rehabilitation leaders must realize that the mental attitude of the patient is of prime importance. In the final analysis, the patient will need to accomplish the objectives. The program and leadership provide the means and encouragement, but actual accomplishment depends on the individual's cooperation.

Rehabilitation work received great impetus from the work done by the armed forces. The number of men who returned from World War II, and succeeding wars, disabled and handicapped drew public attention to their need for assistance.

TYPES OF DISABILITIES

Disability can be categorized as physical, emotional, neurological, and social. Physical disabilities include amputation, cardiac defects, arthritis, orthopedic deformation, blindness, and disorders of speech. Almost half of all patients in hospitals in the United States are suffering from emotionally-related disorders; common categories are neuroses and psychoses, and examples are dementia praecox, schizophrenia, and paranoia. The neurologically disabled include the cerebral palsied, the blind, the deaf, and those with disorders of speech, vision, and hearing, as well as the mentally retarded. Among the socially incapacitated are the criminally insane, sexual deviants, kleptomaniacs, alcoholics, and drug addicts.

In addition to rehabilitation through the military, a great deal more must be done, especially for disabled civilians, if we are to fulfill our responsibility in a democratic society. We should recognize people as individuals, regardless of observable differences. Within the limits of their disabilities, all can and should live bountiful, dignified lives.

MENTAL RETARDATION

For a definition of mental retardation we quote the American Association on Mental Deficiency: "Mental retardation refers to subaverage intellectual functioning which originates during the developmental period, and is associated with impairment or inadaptive behavior."[1] A number of significant criteria emerge as we probe more deeply. Herbert J. Prelim summarizes:[2]

1. Mental retardation originates before the individual's eighteenth birthday.
2. Mental subnormality—an intelligent quotient below 70 or 75—indicates mental retardation.
3. Retardation results in social inadequacy—the inability to meet societal demands.
4. Mental retardation has an organic cause.
5. Mental retardation is incurable.

With the exception of the first criterion, the list is open to questions. On the whole, however, the criteria reflect the thinking of experts on this subject and provide considerable insight into the phenomenon.

Incidence of Mental Retardation

Some experts estimate that 3 percent of the population of the United States are mentally retarded. The figure varies as the criteria for mental retardation are narrowed or broadened. Another variable is socioeconomic status within the community. Whether a person is "trainable" or totally dependent is not influenced significantly by his socioeconomic status. However, socioeconomic factors assume greater significance for those in the educable and "slow learner" categories, the borderline cases. Some of those individuals inherit retardation; the remainder are retarded because of physical and even neurological causes. In regard to such cases, recreation is basically a habilitation process. However, it plays an equally vital role in rehabilitation.

AN EXAMINATION OF PLAY

In analyzing play, we observe that children's games reflect the relationships between parents and children, siblings and friends. Al-

---

[1]Rick F. Heber, *A Manual on Terminology and Classification in Mental Retardation* (monograph supplement to *American Journal of Mental Deficiency*, 2nd ed.), p. 3.

[2]Larry L. Neal, *Recreation's Role in the Rehabilitation of the Mentally Retarded* (Eugene, Ore.: Rehabilitation Research and Training Center, 1970), pp. 9–11.

though at first the primary concern is merely play, it evolves into the quest for winning, an attempt to assert one's ego over others to secure approval from family and friends. The stress in attempting to excel in sports can prove a wearing experience greatly removed from "fun." (We do not deny desirable outcomes from competition, despite the low *recreational* level. However, becoming a victor is inextricably woven into the pattern.) Ultimately, winning may play a minor or nonexistent role, with participation indulged in for the game's sake and for the satisfaction derived from involvement, not from winning. All so-called "play" does not result in "fun" as we know it. Play gives various levels of satisfaction, the highest level being that at which scoring or winning is insignificant.

The handicapped child has fundamentally the same needs and wants as other children. Play is as natural to him as to anyone else. He, too, thirsts for companionship, achievement, and recognition. Significant differences are often imperceptible, residing mainly in the fundamental limitations imposed by the particular handicap.

AN EXAMINATION OF GOALS

Preventive, supportive, and remedial efforts are desired. The school is unquestionably one of the most important factors in helping the child try to achieve optimum development. Individualized physical education can further clinical efforts. In addition, valuable lifetime pursuits such as art, handicrafts, music (instrumental and vocal), debating, current events, and dramatics can be developed. Recreation can supplement as well as complement the efforts of the school. The recreation center can continue the efforts of the school, serving as a laboratory for sharpening or furthering skills learned in school, and expanding on them by teaching additional interests in keeping with the individual's disability.

Our overriding task is to add significance and stimulus to the lives of the handicapped. Every effort should be exerted to enrich their lives. Their lives are often filled with trivia; their impediments may prevent their free movement and integration with others. One of the great dangers is the lack of selectivity toward retardation.

Opportunities to view violence and the sexually suggestive are omnipresent in the mass media. Programs that stress the cultural—better music, dramatic arts, interpretive dancing, and so on—are less common. The droves of cheap magazines, paperbacks, television shows, and movies rely on sex and violence as attention-getters; they call for positive action on the part of parents, educators, and psychiatrists. The restrictions that disabilities impose on the handicapped make him all the more susceptible to these damaging influences.

INTEGRATION IS HIGHLY DESIRABLE

Our goal is to integrate the handicapped into "normative" groups wherever feasible. We need to recognize the individual and expose him to experiences which will allow him freedom of opportunity and a wholesome array of "give-and-take" situations. However, integration is desirable only if it does not interfere with the individual's progress or present situation; a green light from the clinical staff is a necessary prerequisite for such efforts.

The needs of the handicapped are similar to those of normative groups except for their respective maladies. Their handicaps may contribute toward a greater than average degree of frustration, deflated ego, suppression, anxiety, and introspection. It follows that the handicapped have a greater than average need for recreational outlets and therefore stand to benefit more fully from the restorative influences of recreation. Let us examine the physical, emotional and social benefits that may be derived from recreation.

Physical Benefits

Activity is a law of life. The reflexes established by movement affect not only the musculature but also the nerve pathways; skill development and growth are natural consequences. The ingenuity employed by a handicapped person to compensate for his disability is astounding. The motivation provided by physical activity can help achieve responses that would otherwise be impossible. The complete involvement of a mute child in physical activity, for example, can cause him to "explode" with utterances. Similarly, the blind can run, climb, wrestle and swim with abandon.

Physical activities for the atypical must be based on a philosophy. The Bill of Rights for Handicapped Children, product of the White House Conference on Child Health and Protection, states that the handicapped child has a right:

1. To as vigorous a body as human skill can give him.
2. To an education so adapted to his handicap that he can be economically independent and have the chance for the fullest life of which he is capable.

3. To be brought up and educated by those who understand the nature of the burden he has to bear and who consider it a privilege to help him bear it.

4. To grow up in a world which does not set him apart, which looks at him, not with scorn or pity or ridicule—but which welcomes him, exactly as it welcomes every child, which offers him identical privileges and identical responsibilities.

5. To a life on which his handicap casts no shadow but which is full day by day with those things which make it worthwhile, with comradeship, love, work, play, laughter and tears—a life in which these things bring continually increasing growth, richness, release of energies, joy in achievement.

Emotional Benefits

Play revitalizes the life of the handicapped person. He dresses and breakfasts with eagerness so that he will not miss the bus and thereby be deprived of a day of fun. He looks forward to the comradery and satisfactions of the experiences awaiting him. His family is more significant upon his return, for now he has something different to relate to them. He has established an independent life for himself and acquired interests and skills that can be shared with the other members of his family. His ego is inflated and his self-esteem nurtured because he has become a more interesting person to others. Life has taken on a new meaning: recognition, acceptance, expression, and self-fulfillment. Challenging situations and adventure have made his world limitless. Self-assurance has replaced excessive reliance on others.

Social Benefits

Recreation helps the individual experience group situations. The opportunities are limited only by the imagination of the group and its leadership. Activities are the avenues through which the social graces are mastered and friendships developed.

Children handicapped by poliomyelitis will respond to groups differently from those with cerebral palsy, but what is significant is that satisfying social interplay has placed the individual on a volitional level. He is more receptive to the influences of the leader and to the worthwhile experiences that emanate from the group.

A Sample Situation

The situation in Lafayette, Indiana is familiar to one of the authors. If it should strike the reader as a worthy model, so much the better. The dedicated efforts of several people in Lafayette have raised $3,000; the Wabash Center for Mentally Retarded and the United Fund jointly contributed another $3,000; work-study help has contributed the equivalent of an additional $1,500. The fund is administered through the West Lafayette Parks and Recreation Department and an advisory committee. Facilities are provided at the Happy Hollow Park, where the morning portion of the program is conducted, and the Purdue University swimming pool, where the afternoon activities are held. Volunteers augment the paid staff so that a one-to-one leader–child ratio is maintained. In addition, a fine evening program for the adult handicapped is supported by an additional $1,000.

Similar pooling of community should be done in numerous situations where the handicapped are now left to their own devices. While the home is undeniably the starting point, the family is hardly able to cope with the many needs of its handicapped member. Wherever feasible, a room at home should be available for play and exercise. Inviting a playmate to join the activity will usually add to its benefit. An outdoor play area supplied with suitable play equipment is also desirable. The family should be trained how to conduct games and social functions in the home; sample programs and a manual will help. Such a home arrangement can constitute a significant supplement to community-wide efforts.

THE ROLE OF EDUCATION

Recreation and physical education play an important role in rehabilitation. Physical education programs help the individual acquire skills which in turn lead to valuable physical, social, and psychological returns. They also contribute toward his physical conditioning. The value of physical education in rejuvenating muscular tissue is indispensable in the rehabilitation of the physically handicapped. The amputee must learn to use the mechanical devices which will enable him to perform many functions for himself. Physical education plays an important part in such training.

The recreation program, encompassing the entire range of human interest, uses the skills and talents developed in other fields of endeavor; physical skills, music, dramatics, handicrafts, social recreation, camping, hobbies, and special events all contribute to a rich recreation program for the handicapped. Their need to express themselves and achieve fulfillment is great. Allowance should be made for suggestions from the participants themselves.

ANALYSIS OF REHABILITATION

We usually think of rehabilitation as restoring to normal use the physical, mental, and/or social adjustment of an individual. The recreation leader, the physical director, the nurse, and the therapist cannot afford to become too solicitous in their dealings with the patient. He wants no sympathy; it may bring resentment and rebellion. He faces a tough battle which he will win more readily through his own efforts. But he does need help, and that is where the leader's wisdom and tact are important. Skill in dealing with the handicapped calls for both native qualities and training. Recreation for the fun of it should be the approach; it is one of the leading methods of successful rehabilitation. In essence, recreation is used as a therapeutic measure.

The program at Logansport State Hospital, Logansport, Indiana, is an example of what can be done in the rehabilitation of the mentally ill. It includes the following:

1. It motivates the patient through leisure-time experiences.
2. It provides actual community center programming to approximate the patient's "outside" experiences.
3. It involves patients in community leisure activities at centers in surrounding areas.
4. It offers patient leisure counseling before release to ease the transition from institution to community.
5. It conducts actual clubs under the 4-H Home Demonstration program. Upon release, the patient is then transferred to an active club in his community.

THERAPEUTIC MEASURES

Dan Corbin, referring to therapeutic recreation, play therapy, and occupational therapy, states:[3]

Recreational therapy makes use of play media to provide the mentally and/or physically ill with satisfactory interests and outlets in conjunction with the other therapeutic means at hand. It is suited for all age groups and is used as supplemental therapy to promote general well-being and develop social skills as therapy progresses. It is general in nature. In play therapy, we observe techniques that are utilized primarily on children. They are afforded opportunities to play-out their troubles. They express their innermost feelings while being figuratively carried away by the play situations.

[3]H. Dan Corbin, *Recreation Leadership* (3rd ed.) (Englewood Cliffs, N.J.: Prentice-Hall, Inc., 1970), p. 261.

... By means of occupational therapy, an emphasis is placed on the use of handicrafts to help to restore the patient to a state of restored confidence and vocational competence.

Play is good medicine for all, and especially for the bedridden, the emotionally disturbed, and the handicapped. Whenever feasible, play activities should resemble those familiar to the "outside world." An attempt to approximate the "normal" should be made at every opportunity, not only to lend added significance to the activities, but also to contribute toward habilitation or rehabilitation, as the case may be. Self-esteem and ego will be nurtured. Furthermore, the individual's ability to adapt to "halfway" programming will be enhanced.

Camping experiences merit particular mention. The serenity of the outdoors, coupled with thorough appreciation and understanding of nature lore, plants, and animals, can do much to brighten the outlook of those who may be resigned to a restricted regimen.

Note that by "therapy," we mean treatment by some remedial or curative process. Additional benefit can be realized by the patient who engages in the program for the sheer enjoyment of the activities rather than for the therapeutic value. The selection of a therapeutic recreation activity is influenced by the patient's handicap and status. Many forms of recreation are therapeutic for all people; they contribute toward the satisfaction of basic needs and mental and physical health.

The impact of recreation on the handicapped individual's well-being is incalculable. Physical activity brings release, self-expression, and fulfillment vital to everyone. The challenge and the satisfaction of achievement contribute greatly toward development.

We can hardly separate the physical from the nervous and emotional aspects of an activity. Neuromuscular involvement is unavoidably associated with the satisfaction of learning skills and involving in social interplay. Shared experiences, often reduced or prohibited by a handicap, provide essential emotional outlets. Accomplishment elevates self-esteem and confidence.

THE RECREATION THERAPIST

Recreation therapists are employed predominantly by institutions supported by tax sources. State mental hospitals are provided for mentally ill and retarded adults, and special facilities are provided for children. On the federal level, the Veterans Administration employs recreation therapists in its psychiatric as well as general hospitals.

The American Red Cross also employs recreation therapists, some assigned to armed forces hospitals both in the United States and abroad. In the private sector, employment opportunities exist in private hospitals, convalescent homes, and homes for the aged. Many large cities have recreation therapists in their recreation departments to serve the "halfway centers" and coordinate and direct those recently released from mental institutions.

AN ENCOURAGING TREND

Until recently, medical care ceased when the patient left the hospital. From his release until he returned to work, he was on his own to adjust or rehabilitate himself as well as possible. It is encouraging to see the development of professional interest in proper care of such people from bed to job. On the local level, municipal recreation departments should help the individual modulate from institutional to day-to-day living at home. An increasing number of recreation departments are effectively filling this breach in the patient's life, warding off repeated institutionalization.

Institutions are making greater use of community programs and facilities to augment their own. Such programs put patients in a more natural setting, easing the transition from institution to home. A vital purpose of the recreation program is to provide, as an integral phase of the total medical program, a comprehensive, well-balanced, and professionally executed range of recreational activities to meet the interests, needs, and capabilities of all patients. In general, the recreation program has two primary aims: first, to help the doctor make his patients well; second, to make life as satisfying and meaningful as possible for patients who must remain in the hospital for a long period of time. The recreation program is designed to accomplish the following objectives:

1. Help patients adjust to hospital life and medical treatment
2. Contribute to the total social and psychological readjustment of patients.
3. Contribute to the development and maintenance of a normal physical condition during the patient's stay in the hospital.
4. Help accustom patients to their physical limitations and potentialities.
5. Develop interests and skills in so-called "carry-over" activities; that is, activities in which patients may participate safely and beneficially during their stay in the hospital, as well as after their discharge.

6. Provide doctors with opportunities to observe patients' behavior and response to recreational activity.

THE IMPACT OF ACTIVITIES ON REHABILITATION

The mentally retarded lag behind the performance levels of so-called normal children of the same age, but there is evidence that their performance levels can be improved. After only four weeks of a daily program of physical activities, W. O. Corder found significant progress in physical fitness and measured intelligence.[4] Gerald O'Morrow succinctly summarizes the effect recreation can have on all types of handicapped persons:[5]

1. Increase the growth and development of the child
2. Develop a self-image or awareness of self
3. Reduce isolation by building a relationship with others
4. Take the child away from himself or redirect his attention
5. Reestablish constructive self-attitudes
6. Reduce aggression tendencies while at the same time providing for approved outlets for hostility
7. Stimulate interest in new activities
8. Prepare the child for activities of daily living
9. Assist the child to find success
10. Possibly prepare children for adult roles

RECREATIONAL PROGRAMMING

Every effort should be made to expose the participant to a broad spectrum of recreational activities. They may have great impact on normalizing the individual. Recreation should be scheduled periodically, especially when the patient is confined and undergoing the rigors of a rehabilitation regimen. The recreation program should approxi-

[4]W. O. Corder, "Effects of Physical Education on the Intellectual, Physical and Social Development of Educable Mentally Retarded Boys," *Exceptional Children* (Feb. 1966), pp. 357–64.

[5]Gerald O'Morrow, "Physical Education and Recreation for Handicapped Children, Proceedings of a Study Conference," in *The Status of Recreation for Handicapped Children in Institutions* (Washington, D.C.: American Association for Health, Physical Education and Recreation, 1969), pp. 30–31.

mate that of community recreation centers. Some common suitable activities follow:

Archery	Fishing & casting (fly, bait, spin)
Arts and crafts	Horseshoes
Bowling	Volleyball
Swimming	Rhythmics
Softball	Table games
Badminton	Croquet
Camping	Lawn bowls
Tennis	Golf
Music	Games of low organization
Story telling	Dramatics
Stunts and tumbling	Sports
Games of high organization	Special events

Stress should be on activities that can be shared with the nonhandicapped. The need for halfway centers becomes paramount; they can help the institutionalized and those at home to become oriented to "normal" day-to-day enriched involvement.

SUMMARY

Recreation plays a major role in any rehabilitation program. Recreation activities have been used as a therapeutic measure in the treatment of patients and have proven to be a valuable means of achieving desirable results. The greatest value of recreation, above its contribution to the medical care of the patient, is the tremendous emotional and social lift brought by his involvement in the activities.

Selected Reading

AMERICAN ASSOCIATION FOR HEALTH, PHYSICAL EDUCATION AND RECREATION, and NATIONAL RECREATION AND PARK ASSOCIATION, *Physical Education and Recreation for Handicapped Children.* Washington, D.C.: American Association for Health, Physical Education and Recreation, 1969.

BUELL, CHARLES E., *Physical Education for Blind Children.* Springfield, Ill.: Charles C Thomas, Publisher, 1966.

Challenge (journal).

Corbin, H. Dan, *Recreation Leadership* (3rd ed.). Englewood Cliffs, N.J.: Prentice-Hall, Inc., 1970.

Exceptional Children (journal).

Haun, Paul, *Recreation: A Medical Viewpoint,* eds. Elliott M. Avedon and Frances B. Arje. New York: Columbia University, Teachers College, 1965.

Heber, Rick F., *A Manual on Terminology and Classification in Mental Retardation.* Monograph supplement to *American Journal of Mental Deficiency,* 2nd ed., 1961.

Journal of the American Corrective Therapy Association.

Journal of Health, Physical Education and Recreation.

Journal of Leisure Research.

Kirk, Samuel A., *Exceptional Children.* Boston: Houghton Mifflin Company, 1962.

Kraus, Richard, *Recreation Today: Program Planning and Leadership.* New York: Appleton-Century-Crofts, 1966.

Meyer, Harold D., Charles K. Brightbill, and H. Douglas Sessoms, *Community Recreation* (4th ed.). Englewood Cliffs, N.J.: Prentice-Hall, Inc., 1969.

Neal, Larry L., *Recreation's Role in the Rehabilitation of the Mentally Retarded.* Eugene, Ore.: Rehabilitation Research and Training Center, 1970.

Outlook (journal).

Parks and Recreation (journal).

Physical Therapy (journal).

Rathbone, Josephine L., and Carol Lucas, *Recreation in Total Rehabilitation.* Springfield, Ill.: Charles C Thomas, Publisher, 1970.

Research Quarterly (journal).

Rusk, Howard A., and Eugene J. Taylor, *Living with a Disability.* Garden City, N.Y.: The Blakeston Company, Inc., 1953.

Therapeutic Recreation Journal.

chapter nine

RECREATION
IN OTHER
INSTITUTIONS

*As if we could kill time without injuring
eternity.*

HENRY DAVID THOREAU

Any book on recreation should
deal with contributions made by nonpublic recreational institutions. To
a considerable extent, such institutions have been in a position to experiment and innovate. Not dependent on tax support, they can more
easily explore new programming and facilities planning. As a consequence, they have been in the vanguard of recreational progress and
deserve the designation as pioneers in the burgeoning recreation profession.

THE CHURCH

For many years the church was opposed to play and recreation.
This stand was a carry-over from asceticism (self-denial of worldly ex-

periences) and the Puritan Ethic. The attitude that play was sinful belonged not only to the church, but also to the school and to our ancestors. Fortunately, the church, the school, and parents have changed; they now recognize play and recreation as a social force of great potential value for community life. Increasingly, the church recognizes recreation and its place as a community social institution. Many churches conduct well-rounded recreational programs for their members. The various denominations count their members in the millions; we can readily recognize their great opportunity for community service through wholesome recreation programs. Ideally, each church would have a recreation committee with a liaison to coordinate the recreation program to the overall church program. A representative from each of the various churches in the community could serve on a larger committee with members from all the various community institutions and organizations. Such an arrangement would help to organize the total community for recreation.

Efforts of the various groups should be cooperative, not competitive. Overlapping efforts could be prevented by means of a study of the needs of individual groups and the community as a whole.

Leadership

Large churches may be able to afford the services of a professionally qualified recreation leader, whereas small churches may use part-time leadership and/or the services of volunteers. In some instances the public recreation department might employ a qualified leader to work with the churches in the development of their recreation programs. The churches could pay all or part of the salary of this recreation leader. Regardless of the organization and whether the leaders are professional or volunteer, the program should serve all age groups, from the very young to the aged.

Program

The program should be varied enough to meet the needs and interests of all. Athletics, sports, aquatics, games, music, art, dramatics, crafts, and nature programs should be included. Many churches have campsites of their own. Others have facilities such as gymnasiums, auditoriums, or recreation centers, while many temporarily use Sunday school facilities while saving for more elaborate facilities.

Church recreation programs have far surpassed the days of church suppers and Sunday school picnics, now includes activities geared to all members. Church leagues in sports such as basketball and softball are common. Cub Scouts and Brownies, Boy Scouts and Girl Scout groups are frequently organized within the church membership.

The Catholic Church and Recreation

The contributions of the National Catholic Youth Organization (CYO) to the Catholic youth of our country are recognized. Well organized and administered, it has provided a wide and interesting program of activities under wise, understanding, and sympathetic leadership. While it has conducted a strong athletic program, its activities have not been limited to sports. Music, art, dramatics, and social recreation activities are carried out with equal enthusiasm. The craft program in particular is often outstanding. The diversified program of the CYO indicates the high regard of the Catholic Church for the influence of wholesome recreation on our youth.

The Protestant Church and Recreation

The many Protestant churches have also broadened their recreational scope. The various denominations have developed recreation programs on the local level, accompanied by expansion of facilities.

Paid and volunteer leaders have stimulated diversified recreational opportunities. Church athletic leagues have been established all over the country. Church choral groups are numerous. Even small neighborhood churches have recreation committees to conduct programs for their members.

The Mormon Church

The Church of Jesus Christ of the Latter-Day Saints (Mormon) conducts one of the most comprehensive church recreation programs. Its Young Women's Mutual Improvement Association emphasizes the emotional, intellectual, social, and spiritual growth of those between twelve and twenty-six. Its male counterpart operates a comparable association for young men. The two associations function independently though they join together for activity programs, with the exception of sports, athletics, and camping. Common areas of activity are dance, drama, music, speech, athletics for young men, and sports and camp for young women. Under the aegis of the Young Men's Mutual Improvement Association Scouts experience camping activities.

The YMCA

The Evangelical Protestant churches founded the YMCA for the purpose of teaching religious doctrine and providing a religious environment for youth. The idea, originated by George Williams, an English dry-goods clerk, has spread over the world. Founded about the middle of the nineteenth century, the YMCA soon recognized the value of recreational activities and included gymnasiums in the building plans of its facilities. To provide trained Christian leadership to direct the program of physical education and recreation, the YMCA decided in 1885 to erect an educational institution, and established the International YMCA Training School at Springfield, Massachusetts. Now known as Springfield College, it has been training young men not only for service in the YMCA but also in schools, colleges, and universities throughout the world for over sixty years. It has broadened its scope in areas of study and opened its doors to young women interested in recreation leadership.

Physical education and recreation are deeply rooted in the YMCA program. The influence of this program on our youth has been such that its continuance should be our concern. In some cases public recreation has come to a community and the administrator of the public program has said to the YMCA, "You have done a grand job for the community, for which we all thank you. Now we will take over." This is a faulty conception of community organization for recreation; there is always a definite place for the YMCA and all the other youth-serving organizations. It is the responsibility of the superintendent of public recreation to set up the machinery for recreation within the community. All the local institutions and organizations can contribute to a rich leisure-time program. Division of efforts will result in savings to the taxpayer.

The YWCA

The YWCA serves through its contribution to the young women of the world just as the YMCA serves the young men. While its operation may not be as extensive, it has the same ideals as the YMCA and offers a similar program. Recreation programs play an important part in the work of the YWCA. Its buildings in large cities contain gymnasiums, studios, swimming pools, reading rooms, and so on, and it may run summer camps for young women's weekends and/or summer vacations.

The YMHA and YWHA

Under the sponsorship of the Jewish Welfare Board, the Young Men's Hebrew Association and the Young Women's Hebrew Association serve Jewish youth through numerous community centers. Recreation, in addition to religious activities, plays an important part of their overall program. Like the YMCA and YWCA, the YMHA and YWHA are an educational force in the communities in which they are situated.

BOY SCOUTS

The Boy Scout movement has been highly valuable to communities throughout the world. Scouts are held to high standards of conduct and service. The Scouting program, rich in experiences of the outdoors, nature study, camping, and campcraft, brings satisfactions vital for normal growth and development during a particularly impressionable period of a boy's life. Facilities in different localities may vary, but the Scout camp is always present, either through direct ownership or cooperative arrangement with some other agency. Boy Scouts are eleven through eighteen years of age and Explorers, fourteen through twenty; handicapped boys may stay in Boy Scouts beyond age eighteen.

The Cub Scouts

Younger boys from eight to eleven respect their older brothers. They hope to be Scouts some day, and Cub Scouts prepares them for entering the Boy Scout organization while it fulfills their present needs. Recreation is an important part of Cub Scouting. Each Cub den, under adult guidance, provides recreational experiences.

GIRL SCOUTS

What we have said of Boy Scouts applies equally to Girl Scouts. Rich recreation programs meet the needs of girls in the Scout age group. Activities are arranged with the needs and interests of the girls in mind. Girl Scout camps provide camping experiences that leave a lasting impression on girls who have belonged to the Scouts. Through its recreational opportunities, the Girl Scout organization also contributes to community recreation services.

The Brownies

Like the Cub Scouts, the Brownies organization meets the needs of younger girls. Brownies helps develop an awareness of ideals, standards of conduct, and international goodwill. The thrill of visits to campsites and other excursions are valuable experiences for these girls. As they learn to *play* with other people, they also learn to *live* with them.

CAMP FIRE GIRLS

The Camp Fire Girls also have a rich recreation program for young girls. Founded by Dr. and Mrs. Luther Gulick in 1910, it is composed of three groups: Blue Birds (seven to ten years), Camp Fire Girls (ten to fifteen), and Horizon Clubs (fifteen to eighteen years). Camp Fire Girls also teaches and upholds high standards of conduct. Camping is a vital part of its program, with great emphasis on individual needs.

OTHER YOUTH-SERVING ORGANIZATIONS

Numerous other organizations contribute to education for leisure and the development of high standards of conduct, for example, the American Junior Red Cross, Boys Clubs of America, Future Farmers of America, Future Homemakers of America, American Youth Hostels, Hi-Y and Junior Hi-Y, and the Youth Division of the National Social Welfare Assembly.

CIVIC ORGANIZATIONS

Many civic organizations contribute to leisure-time programs for young people. The Rotary, Kiwanis, Lions, Optimists, Exchange, and other service organizations sponsor picnics, swimming meets, and other recreational activities for youths in their communities. Many such organizations sponsor extensive summer camp programs in their localities. Other community organizations, such as the Parent-Teachers Association, the American Legion, the Junior Chamber of Commerce, and the Federation of Business and Professional Women's Clubs, also contribute to leisure-time programs for children and adults. These organizations are interested in civic improvement and greater opportunity for the growth and development of youth.

The press and radio stations in many communities also contribute to leisure-time programs by sponsoring picnics, track meets, carnivals, and other recreational events.

COMMERCIAL RECREATION

A recreation facility owned and operated for profit is classified as commercial recreation. Many types of commercial recreation help the leisure needs of communities. It is important, however, to determine that the activities are conducted under conditions which benefit society. Regardless of how acceptable an activity may appear, the environment under which it is conducted can make it wholly undesirable.

We should resist the tendency to scorn commerical enterprises, although we should ensure that they are properly controlled. Wholesome commercial enterprises deserve our encouragement and support. We not only accept but practically demand certain types of commercial recreation, such as theaters, concert halls, amusement parks, night clubs, pool and billiard halls, and bowling alleys. To be sure, opinion on the value of some of them may be divided. Often, it is not the nature of the activities that condemns them, but the manner in which the establishment is run and the standards of behavior which are considered tolerable. Each community should establish acceptable standards and licensing practices compatible with recognized codes of behavior. Commercial recreation should be part of the total leisure-time program, represented in community program planning.

SUMMARY

Many different institutions exist for the betterment of society, and most of them involve planning for the wise use of leisure time. All of these institutions should recognize the importance of coordinating their efforts, among themselves and with various well-regulated commercial recreational ventures. Together, all can contribute to enriched leisure-time offerings for the community.

Suggested Reading

BRIGHTBILL, CHARLES K., *Man and Leisure: A Philosophy of Recreation.* Englewood Cliffs, N.J.: Prentice-Hall, Inc., 1961.

CLEMENS, FRANCES, ROBERT TULLY, and EDWARD CRILL, *Recreation and the Local Church.* Elgin, Ill.: Brethren Publishing Company, 1958.

DULLES, FOSTER RHEA, *A History of Recreation: America Learns to Play,* 2nd ed. New York: Appleton-Century-Crofts, 1966.

FEDERAL SECURITY AGENCY, *Youth Centers: An Appraisal and a Look Ahead.* Washington, D.C.: U.S. Government Printing Office, 1945.

HJELTE, GEORGE, and JAY S. SHIVERS, *Public Administration of Park and Recreational Services.* New York: The Macmillan Company, 1963.

KAPLAN, MAX, *Leisure in America: A Social Inquiry.* New York: John Wiley & Sons, Inc., 1960.

MEYER, HAROLD D., CHARLES K. BRIGHTBILL, and H. DOUGLAS SESSOMS, *Community Recreation: A Guide to Its Organization.* Englewood Cliffs, N.J.: Prentice-Hall, Inc., 1969.

MILLER, NORMAN, and DUANE ROBINSON, *The Leisure Age.* Belmont, Calif.: Wadsworth Publishing Co., Inc., 1963.

PYLAND, AGNES DURANT, *Church Recreation.* Nashville, Tenn.: Convention Press, 1959.

SMITH, JULIAN, REYNOLD CARLSON, GEORGE DONALDSON, and HUGH MASTERS, *Outdoor Education*, 2nd ed. Englewood Cliffs, N.J.: Prentice-Hall, Inc., 1972.

THOMPSON, VICTOR A., *Modern Organization*. New York: Alfred A. Knopf, Inc., 1961.

"YOU *HEARD* THE RANGER! THE PARK IS *FULL! OVERFLOWING!*"

chapter ten

RECREATION
ON THE FEDERAL
AND STATE LEVELS

*Constructive and creative use of leisure is
becoming a worldwide influence in building
better understanding between peoples.*

U THANT

THE FEDERAL GOVERNMENT AND
RECREATION

The United States government, established on the principles of
equality of opportunity and individual rights, has demonstrated its concern for the welfare of the people. Many of its bureaus and departments
are engaged in providing recreational opportunities for the public.

The federal government's role in providing recreational opportunities is little known, primarily because no single bureau or department
is totally concerned with recreation. Agencies whose major responsibility is something other than recreation cannot be expected to publicize
both. It would be difficult to determine how well informed people are
about the recreational opportunities provided by the federal government; many people know nothing about them. Relatively few people
take advantage of these opportunities. More unified and effective publicity is necessary, both to educate people about the opportunities and

to develop their interest in recreation. School programs could be enhanced through use of the services of the federal bureaus, such as illustrated literature, motion pictures, and slides about national forests, parks, and monuments.

The Department of Health, Education and Welfare consists of five principle units: the Social Security Administration, the Public Health Service, the Food and Drug Administration, the Office of Vocational Rehabilitation, and the Office of Education. HEW might easily include a division of recreation, too. Some people feel that the Division of Recreation should be under the Office of Education; others contend that recreation and the leisure-time arts are important enough for recognition and attention equal to that given to the five main units. Still others staunchly support the advisability of a separate recreation department with cabinet rank. They aver that increasing affluence and expanding leisure go hand in hand. Consequently, we need to coordinate federal efforts concerning recreation.

Agencies, Bureaus, and Their Services

The United States government agencies and bureaus described below are only a few of recreation-related federal efforts. An exhaustive treatment of the topic would demand more space than a text of this scope can allot.

Administration on Aging. The Administration on Aging is part of the Department of Health, Education and Welfare and functions under the Older Americans Act. Its funds trickle down to state government agencies for construction, purchase, and repairs of recreational facilities. Under Titles III and IV of the act; salaries may be authorized for planning, administering, and directing recreational activities.

Army Corps of Engineers. Ostensibly concerned with maintaining flood control and navigational waterways, the Army Corps of Engineers serves recreational objectives as well, for example, boat launching and docking.

Bureau of the Census. In addition to counting and describing the characteristics of our population, the Bureau of the Census compiles data on the amounts expended on and the revenues gathered from recreation and leisure-related enterprises.

Bureau of Outdoor Recreation. Established as an outgrowth of the Outdoor Recreation Resources Review Commission in 1962, the Bureau of Outdoor Recreation is part of the Department of the Interior. It administers the Land and Water Conservation funds, matching state funds for distribution to municipalities and counties. These funds are used for the planning, purchase, and development of publicly owned and administered recreation facilities.

Children's Bureau. Created for the purpose of improving the condition of children's welfare, the Children's Bureau has made definite contributions in the field of recreation.

Cooperative Agricultural Extension Service. The conditions of rural life have changed with the mechanization of farm work and added leisure time. Improved roads and means of transportation have resulted in increased communication between country and city. The mass media, education, and economic progress have also raised living standards for residents of rural areas. The Cooperative Agricultural Extension Service (involving agricultural extension departments of land-grant colleges and the United States Department of Agriculture) has kept abreast of the times and contributed effectively toward the development of recreation areas, facilities, and programs for the rural population.

Land-grant colleges and universities in the United States have helped to educate the rural population for wholesome use of leisure. Their sociologists and recreation leaders give guidance and assistance in the development of diversified recreation programs.

Recreation is also a vital part of 4-H club programs. As long ago as 1919, 4-H encouraged projects in wildlife and nature lore, and in the early 1920s music programs were added. Many people believe that 4-H programming is directed exclusively at the rural population. The Annual 4-H Youth Development Enrollment Report,[1] covering the period from 1 July 1970 to 30 June 1971 in Indiana, proves the truth to be different from their impression. Of the 113,535 participants in 4-H, a significant number were drawn from towns and cities of 10,000 or more people.

Farms	34,681	Suburbs of city of over 50,000	15,048
Towns under 10,000 and open country	33,655	Central city of over 50,000	19,371
Towns and cities 10,000 to 50,000	10,780	Total	113,535

[1]Edward L. Frickey, *Annual 4-H Youth Development Enrollment Report* (West Lafayette, Ind.: Cooperative Extension Service, Purdue University, 1971).

Farmers Home Administration. Part of the Department of Agriculture, the Farmers Home Administration makes loans to individual farmers, public bodies, and nonprofit groups in communities under 5,500 in population for recreation. It will lend up to 100 percent of the purchase price of lands for specific recreation purposes and for the development of certain types of facilities. Interest rates are 5 percent or less, and repayment must be made within forty years.

Fish and Wildlife Service. The contribution of this federal agency is probably better known than that of any of the others, because millions of people hunt and fish in the United States each year. The Fish and Wildlife Service cooperates with many state departments.

Forest Service. The Forest Service provides areas and facilities in the national forests for hiking, camping, winter sports, swimming, riding, hunting, and scenic drives. Rangers assist in directing activities when and where this is advisable. They assign people to particular areas, give safety instructions and to some extent serve as recreation leaders.

Housing Assistance Administration. Although this agency is primarily concerned with the construction of houses for families with low incomes, it is naturally also concerned with the welfare of the people who will live there. The construction of recreation facilities in housing developments is part of its job. It provides technical assistance for facilities development and establishing standards for recreation.

National Park Service. The number of people who visit national parks increases each year. The parks possess historic interest, scientific interest, or scenic value, and often all three. Many provide hotel services, lodges, and cabins for visitors. Depending on the location and the season of the year, fishing, camping, hiking, boating, swimming, picnicking, and winter sports may be available.

Office of Education. The United States Office of Education is a service agency to education throughout the nation. While education for leisure is one of its major objectives, little service has been rendered in this field. The Office of Education should play a more major part in developing physical education, music, dramatics, and art programs as part of education for leisure.

Renewal Assistance Administration. This agency makes grants (better known as Open-Space Funds, directly to states and local governments to expedite land acquisition in urban areas. Its intent is to stimulate long-range planning for recreation and conservation areas.

Soil Conservation Service. Consistent with soil conservation practices, this agency stimulates outdoor recreational pursuits such as picnicking, camping, fishing, boating, and hunting. It shares the costs of sanctioned fish and wildlife reserves and public recreation facilities.

Federal Organizations during Emergencies

The Works Progress Administration. During the Depression, the government made an effort to provide employment for the many people who needed work. Many different projects were established, among them one in recreation.

The WPA had the stigma of poverty attached to it from the start. Government regulations allowed only 5 percent of all its personnel to be classified as administrators, free from qualification on the basis of relief. In other words, to work on the WPA you had to take a poverty oath unless you were on the administrative staff.

The public never fully realized the WPA's great contribution to the health, happiness, and welfare of the people of the United States. Before 1934 approximately 34,000 people were employed in the field of recreation leadership. By the fall of 1934 the figure had risen to 40,000. Before the advent of the WPA, recreation programs consisted primarily of athletics and sports; few organized programs in music, dramatics, or arts and crafts were provided. These were referred to as the "neglected areas of recreation," and the WPA emphasized their development. Before the WPA, the only organized agency that trained recreation leaders professionally was the National Recreation Association, which had a one-year school for students with baccalaureate degrees and an interest in recreation as a profession. The WPA was instrumental in encouraging the construction of recreation facilities in many communities in the United States. The PWA (Public Works Administration), part of the WPA, constructed these facilities. Both organizations made lasting contributions to recreation programs and facilities in the United States.

United Services Organizations

During World War I military administrators learned the dangers of unorganized effort to entertain servicemen during their leisure time. There seemed to be a competitive attitude among service organizations, and in some cases undesirable situations resulted. The federal government was instrumental in bringing about the incorporation of six prominent agencies into the United Service Organizations, Inc.: the Young Men's Christian Association, the Young Women's Christian Association, the National Catholic Community Service, the Salvation Army, the Jewish Welfare Board, and the National Travelers' Aid Association.

The USO rendered extremely valuable service during World War II, both at home and abroad. Its primary purpose was to provide recreational opportunity for members of the armed forces who were off duty or on leave. USO centers in communities adjacent to military installations provided dances, games, sports, and other forms of wholesome recreation. Facilities for writing letters, reading, and listening to good music, as well as visits in private homes with family groups, were all part of the USO program. USO Camp Shows, Inc. provided talented entertainment to American servicemen stationed throughout the world, at the request of special service and commanding officers.

The American National Red Cross. We are familiar with the work of the Red Cross in calamities and disasters of all kinds. We may not know that the Red Cross also provides recreation facilities and opportunities in leave and on-post areas overseas at the request of the military. It also renders its recreational services in hospitals at home and abroad. The Red Cross goes where it is needed, even to remote areas where discomfort is great (and its services more coveted).

The Salvation Army. The valuable services of the Salvation Army include aiding men with social, emotional, and spiritual needs; arranging work therapy programs; caring for unwed mothers and their infants at maternity homes and hospitals; maintaining settlements and day care centers; providing emergency disaster service; and aiding prisoners and parolees with counseling, employment assistance, and material aid.

The Salvation Army serves in seventy countries and maintains close to 20,000 charitable centers. In Vietnam, it relieves suffering through welfare services and medical clinics. Recreational activities and all-family involvement are part of its programs.

RECREATION IN BRANCHES OF THE
MILITARY

The Air Force. To provide leisure-time activities for all its personnel and their families, the Air Force has prescribed the Special Services Program, which includes sports, crafts and hobbies, youth activities, special interest groups, motion pictures, service clubs and entertainment, rest centers and recreation areas, and libraries. The base Special Services officer is responsible for implementing, operating, and evaluating an on- and off-base recreation program for personnel and their families. He must continually analyze personnel interests, resources, and facilities. He plans budgetary requirements for recreational facilities, including the base exchange, open messes, airmen's clubs, and day rooms. He is also expected to cooperate with local civic and recreation organizations to supplement on-base recreation programs. Community members may be used as leaders to conduct off-base activities.

The Army. Through its Special Services Division, the Army provides its personnel with programs, services, and facilities to meet their leisure-time needs, at stations within the continental limits of the United States and overseas. Among the program features are handicrafts, music, motion pictures, sports, games, theatrical events, and dancing. While the service club is usually the hub of the program, off-base facilities are often used.

The place of recreation in leisure time and its contribution toward personal adjustment are particularly significant when adjustment is sought under trying and even terrifying conditions. Sports and games, both intra- and extramural, play a prominent role. Outstanding performers sometimes compete in the Olympics and the Pan American Games.

The Marine Corps. The Personnel Department is responsible for recreational programming within the Marine Corps. Morale and fitness are a major concern. In war zones, rest-and-recuperation services for Marine personnel are a prime feature of its programming. (This is equally true of the Army and the Navy). In Vietnam, servicemen are eligible for a five-day "R and R" trip annually to one of nine Oriental cities.

For the Marines, as well as for other service branches, American Red Cross hostesses conduct social programs in the field as well as library and film services. Marines' Special Services are administered at the headquarters, with the responsibility for each unit vested in the local commander.

The Navy. The Navy's recreational services are also handled by its Special Services Division, whose objective is to bolster and maintain morale among Navy personnel. The program resembles to a considerable extent those of the Air Force and Army. The one significant difference is the result of the more restricted life on shipboard. To be sure, aircraft carriers can program activities that require an open space as large as an athletic field! However, library services, physical fitness programs, movies, and self-education are more prominent in the Naval regimen of Special Services.

RECREATION AT THE STATE LEVEL

State Interagency Committees

Several states have organized interagency committees composed of representatives from the various state departments that render some form of recreation service. These interagency committees are often organized through the combined efforts of the National Recreation Association and representatives of one of the state departments.

The interagency committee is a step toward achieving greater cooperation and coordination of effort among agencies and departments. Avoidance or reduction of duplicated effort is a primary objective, along with greater efficiency and enhancement of services. These committees contain members from such agencies as health, highway, library, education, agricultural extension service, youth conservation commission, division of health, physical education and recreation, forestry and conservation, and fish and wildlife service.

Interagency committees are not the panacea for all of recreation's ailments. They cannot realistically be expected to serve as effectively as a single department or agency devoted exclusively to the vital aim of providing diversified recreational activities throughout the state. North Carolina, Vermont, and California, have had state departments of recreation for some time, and have served as models for other states. The recreation profession and its services are important enough to warrant a separate department devoting its undivided attention to problems of recreation.

State Parks

The development of recreation facilities in state parks has increased the opportunity for individuals and groups to camp, fish, hike, ski, and commune with nature. Many state parks have special features of interest, such as historical museums. In Louisiana, for example, Evangeline State Park in what is referred to as "Evangeline Country" is rich in the lore of the time the Arcadians settled there in their trek from Nova

Scotia. The Audubon State Park is rich in memories of Audubon's life and work in Louisiana.

Other State Agencies

State Fish and Wildlife Service. This state department works with its federal counterpart in improving hunting and fishing conditions in the states, partly by establishing game reserves for the protection and conservation of game. State laws to control hunting and fishing are important in maintaining desirable hunting and fishing conditions, and should be rigidly enforced.

State Art Commission, Department of Education, Youth Commission, and Parks. These and several other state departments are specifically concerned with recreational activities. Their efforts should be coordinated by a state director of recreation. This important objective alone warrants the creation of a state department of recreation.

State Institutions for the Handicapped, Dependent, and Delinquents. Recreation for the handicapped (including the physically handicapped, the mentally defective, and the diseased) is included in the programs of state institutions ranging from prisons, workhouses, reformatories, and detention homes to orphanages, homes for the aged, and schools for the deaf and the blind. This is not an all-inclusive list, but it indicates the attention society is paying to the institutionalized population. It also emphasizes the need to recognize our obligation to people who need special care.

In schools for the deaf and the blind, education for leisure is an objective as important as any other; indeed, it may be much more significant to the deaf and blind than to nonhandicapped students. In institutions of correction, the recreation program should be considered an educative process and should encourage individual social rehabilitation.

Recreation programs in institutions should acknowledge individual differences, skills, attitudes, and appreciations. Music, art, crafts, sports, games, dramatics, nature activities, reading, and special interest group activities should be available. Volunteer leaders can be used to good purpose. In any recreation program, leadership is the most important aspect; it is of even greater importance in recreation that aims to accomplish rehabilitation, whether physical, mental, or social. State institutions, including those for adult and juvenile lawbreakers, should have the financial support necessary to provide a rich recreational program.

SUMMARY

The federal government has contributed to public leisure programs for years. Overlapping and duplication of services have occurred, and in many instances improvement in organization and administration is in order. In many instances, the benefits of long-range planning are obscured by uncoordinated efforts. Many authorities in the field of recreation believe that the establishment of a separate federal recreation department with a qualified staff is highly desirable. Such a department would have the responsibility of advising the states and their political subdivisions and nongovernmental organizations, providing technical information upon request, and giving other assistance on professional matters.

The work that is done in the armed forces, the Veterans Administration hospitals, and penal institutions reflects federal efforts to provide recreational opportunity for those who are government-employed or institutionalized. The states are serving their people through agencies such as the interagency committees, state parks, the fish and wildlife service, land-grant colleges and universities, and the cooperative extension service.

Educators in the areas of sociology, psychology, physical education, and political science are recognizing the absolute need for recreational opportunities in our modern society.

Suggested Reading

ADRIAN, C. R., *State and Local Governments,* 2nd ed. New York: McGraw-Hill Book Company, 1967.

FEDERAL INTERAGENCY COMMITTEE ON RECREATION, *The Role of the Federal Government in the Field of Recreation.* Washington, D.C.: Federal Interagency Committee on Recreation, 1961.

HJELTE, GEORGE, and JAY S. SHIVERS, *Public Administration of Park and Recreational Services.* New York: The Macmillan Company, 1963.

JOHNSON, CLAUDIUS O., *American State and Local Government,* 4th ed. New York: Thomas Y. Crowell Company, 1965.

MEYER, HAROLD D., CHARLES K. BRIGHTBILL, and H. DOUGLAS SESSOMS, *Community Recreation: A Guide to Its Organization.* Englewood Cliffs, N.J.: Prentice-Hall, Inc., 1969.

NATIONAL RECREATION AND PARK ASSOCIATION, *Recreation and Park Yearbook,* 42nd ed. Washington, D.C.: National Recreation and Park Association, 1967.

OUTDOOR RECREATION RESOURCES REVIEW COMMISSION, *Outdoor Recreation for America.* Washington, D.C.: U.S. Government Printing Office, 1962.

RODNEY, LYNN S., *Administration of Public Recreation.* New York: The Ronald Press Company, 1964.

SMITHEE, KENNETH J., *Federal Assistance for Recreation and Parks.* Washington, D.C.: National Recreation and Parks Association, 1967.

chapter eleven

EDUCATION
FOR LEISURE
THROUGH
CULTURAL PURSUITS

*Every man feels instinctively that all the
beautiful sentiments in the world weigh less
than a single lovely action.*

JAMES RUSSELL LOWELL

The home is the most impor-
tant institution in our civilization. Its influence on society is vital. As life
has become more and more complex, the responsibility of the home has
increased, magnifying the problems confronting parents. Many find
themselves incapable of coping with these problems, and the result has
been "the disintegration of the American home." Society has attempted
to meet this dilemma by transferring certain responsibilities from the
home to other institutions such as schools, the church, government
agencies, and youth-serving organizations.

Noting the expanded services of these progressive organizations and
institutions, many parents feel that they have been relieved of the
responsibilities of directing the growth and development of their children. Of course, this conclusion is false. The home remains the most
vital and dynamic force in the development of a child. Admittedly,
parents need assistance from other institutions; however, the problems

facing society will be overcome only through the *combined* efforts of all the agencies and institutions of society.

Education for parenthood, including education for leisure, must be included in the school curriculum. Many institutions are presently attempting to provide what might be termed "in-service training" for parents in meeting the needs of their children. The first step is for parents to recognize that the solution to their problems center around the home; other institutions can only be supportive.

RELIGION

Religion is a powerful force in any societal order. Sunday School can become an integral part of a child's educational experiences. When the child is old enough to understand church services, they can readily become a part of his normal existence. Prayers at night and grace at mealtime can give him a significant feeling of devotion to God. Religion as part of home and family life is accepted by our society.

Religious background affects the individual's total life pattern. The expression, "Tell me what you do in your leisure time and I will tell you what you are," reflects the relationship between character and recreation. Use of leisure time is governed to a certain extent by one's religious beliefs. A religious home atmosphere can be an essential part of the development of character. The religious beliefs and practices of the family group, in addition to the interaction between family members with lay and clerical leaders, is part of the foundation for character development.

Parental overemphasis on religion may result in antagonism and rebellion, destroying the desired outcomes of religious instruction. By precept and example, children are best led into patterns of thought and behavior characteristic of the good life.

Leisure-time pursuits should reflect strength of character and consideration for others. Wholesome relationships with mates, sportsmanship in games and contests, fairness with opponents, and respect for authority are characteristics of well-adjusted youngsters. All these personality traits can be fostered by thoughtful training regardless of religious faith. The Golden Rule is incorporated in Protestantism, Catholicism, and Judaism, as well as in Confucianism, Buddhism, Hinduism, Mohammedanism, and Sikhism.

OUTDOOR EDUCATION

Children will love the out-of-doors naturally if they are given the opportunity. Increasing urbanization and overcrowded cities may make contact with nature difficult, but will often magnify the child's desire to be out-of-doors. Parents who enjoy the out-of-doors will find a way to develop this love in their children. Children whose parents are not outdoorsmen may have to rely on a private or school-run camp.

Public recreation departments, churches, youth-serving agencies, and private enterprises conduct camping programs to meet the needs of youth. Trips to city, state, or national parks are valuable.

Fishing can be easily and enjoyably mastered by the young; its suitability as a family activity is apparent. Hiking helps parent and child alike enjoy scenic beauty, become familiar with fauna and flora, and gaining healthful, invigorating experiences in the out-of-doors. Learning about birds, their habits, and where and how they build their nests will fascinate children. Squirrels and rabbits are equally interesting. Identifying trees by examining their leaves can also be challenging. Visits to the zoo, museum, and aquarium are always fascinating and educational.

Picnics and cookouts are invariably enjoyable and should be a common practice. Learning how to build and care for camp fires is essential. Knowing how to care for oneself in the woods is a skill of lifelong value.

Day camp programs offered by many public recreation departments are excellent means of outdoor education. School camps in many locations contribute greatly to this educational experience. Parents, however, should not ignore their responsibility in this field; not all children have the opportunity to attend day camp, nor do all schools have outdoor education programs.

EDUCATION FOR LEISURE IN MUSIC

Because we are limited by space, we shall consider musical activities as an example of a popular cultural pursuit. A similar approach can be used for art, dance, dramatics, language arts, and selected hobbies.

Rhythm

Rhythm is characteristic of life; the infant responds to rhythm before he can walk. Music, with its rhythm and tonal variations, should be part of a child's home environment. He should hear music with strongly accented rhythms: marches such as "Stars and Stripes Forever" and sprightly music such as "Turkey in the Straw." Children respond to lilting songs such as "Yankee Doodle" and "Ten Little Indians," which can introduce them to the satisfaction and enjoyment of music. His first response to rhythm is primarily physical: he attempts to keep time with his feet, body, or fingers. Later, he will begin to listen and respond emotionally.

Melody

Melody has emotional appeal; it involves listening from within and tends to stay in the mind. A child who listens to a melody will soon attempt to hum the tune. Later, he learns the words and tries to sing the song. Melodies of the great masters are available on recordings. Patriotic songs provide melody and stimulate fervor. Folk songs and ballads are excellent material for the child's introduction to the joys of music.

Musical Toys

Musical toys with the characteristics of actual instruments are excellent for developing the child's interest in instrumental music. Enjoying toy drum, xylophone, trumpet, or ocarina may lead to his playing the real instrument. The harmonica is an instrument on which he can learn simple tunes. Manufacturers are now making more elaborate musical toys of higher musical quality, which are nearer to the real thing.

Hand-made Musical Instruments

Making musical instruments is a favorite craft project in many public recreation programs, and it can be done at home as well, with a little ingenuity on the part of the parent. Children can learn to play scales on glasses, tumblers, bottles, or combinations of all three. Shading of tone results from adding water. Each glass or "note" can be identified by using bottle water colors. Flutes and whistles can be made from bamboo; drums can be made from any type of container from a gallon can to an oil drum. It is best to stretch leather tightly over the can and lace it firmly, but the drum head can also be made of shellacked linen or some other cloth; as the shellac dries, it tightens the cloth into a drum head.

The cigar-box violin is well known; homemade banjos and ukeleles can also be a source of considerable fun. Homemade xylophones are made of wooden slabs whittled to varying degrees of thickness and length to produce different tones. Tambourines are not difficult to make, and gourds can be used as percussion instruments.

When children use homemade musical instruments, musical talent can be discovered early and given an opportunity to develop. Even if the child is not particularly talented, he has an opportunity to satisfy some of his basic needs: response to rhythm and melody.

Family Sings

Singing favorite songs together encourages family happiness and solidarity. Holidays take on added significance when celebrated with appropriate songs. Music is a pleasing feature of any celebration.

Children should be introduced to music early in their lives and encouraged to develop an appreciation for music. As John Redman says in his song, "The Man with the Mandolin," "Open up your heart and let the music in."

FAMILY GAMES

The home has traditionally been the center of entertainment, either for the immediate family or for friends and neighbors, too. Quilting parties, corn husking, popping corn, dancing, and singing were traditional group activities.

The countless games suitable for the entire family can bring enjoyment and increased unity. Many board games, such as Monopoly and Scrabble, can be enjoyed by almost all ages, as can card games and puzzles. Children enjoy magic tricks; amateur magicians (fathers) will fascinate them by the hour.

Families that do not play together are not fully unified. Parents who seldom or never play with their children rarely know them completely. Amusing incidents that occur during family playtime can linger as recollections of a happy childhood. Joy and happiness are basic needs which should be satisfied in childhood to ensure the growth of a normal and well-adjusted adult.

HOME OPPORTUNITIES AND INFLUENCES

Many factors encourage the development of skill in music, dramatics, dancing, athletics, and related accomplishments. It is difficult to account for the diversity of children's interests. They should be given opportunities to explore the full range of leisure activities. They are cheated if deprived of these stimulating experiences during their formative years.

Many activities can be conducted at home, in a game room or in the yard. Table tennis, badminton, shuffleboard are popular sports suitable for the yard or driveway. Basketball hoops are common yard and driveway fixtures. Children can learn to catch and throw baseballs and footballs in the yard or on school playgrounds. Many a tennis player has learned his strokes while hitting the ball against the side of a garage. Bait- and fly-casting can be learned in the yard.

A multiple sports area in an ordinary back yard can include a basketball hoop, a trapeze, a blank wall for throwing or hitting against, an open area for croquet, a portable ping pong table, and badminton posts. The dividend realized from the area exceeds the cost and effort expended in arranging it. The greatest motivation to participate in recreational activities is skill: develop a child's skill in an activity and he is "off and running."

In congested city areas where homes have no yards, public recreation departments must provide play areas. Even where open space is common, many children are not given parental recreational guidance, and their potential for learning activities and developing skills is apt to remain undeveloped. Recreational areas under professional leadership are a vital part of any community's planning.

Facilitating the Child's Adjustment

The assistance parents can give their children in adjusting at school and on the playground should not be neglected. A child needs to learn to get along with his classmates and playmates. The preschool child who learns to play with his brothers, sisters, and playmates is acquiring characteristics necessary for proper orientation toward school. Much of his fundamental social training evolves through play attitudes learned during childhood. When a child is deprived of desirable home training, the burden of trying to correct the situation generally falls on the schools. Proper education for leisure in the home could obviate much of the school's work in correction or rehabilitation.

MISCELLANEOUS LEISURE-TIME ACTIVITIES

Homemade Kites

Making kites is challenging and interesting. The Chinese have historically excelled in kite-making; their efforts are worthy of study. Many people today make kites as a hobby and receive great satisfaction from their skill in construction and design. A recent kite-flying contest conducted by a public recreation department exhibited a wide variety of kites. Contest regulations stipulated that the kites were to be made by the contestants with assistance only from their parents. One miniature kite three inches long and one and one-half inches wide could actually fly. Another, the life-size shape of a man, drew considerable attention. Cooperative effort on the part of parent and child was a prime objective of the project. Kite-making is an excellent association of parent and child in a recreational pursuit.

Gardening

Children love to plant things, although many are not eager to care for gardens once they are planted. However, the self-discipline necessary for the success of the garden is surely worth the effort. With a certain amount of encouragement, the parent can help see the activity through. Many elementary schools have garden plots, built with the cooperation of parents.

Tinkering

Children enjoy tinkering with things. Small children take apart and put together toys. Older youngsters often make, fix, or build things. A tool kit and a box of scrap lumber will usually make them as happy as an expensive toy, providing many hours of enjoyable and educational activity.

Experts in child behavior recognize the value to children of the destruction of certain playthings such as broken alarm clocks and household implements. Unless extreme, destruction need not cause undue alarm. The child's destructive tendencies should be channeled toward items that are practically valueless. Such playthings will enable him to express his destructive feelings. Virginia Axline discusses this phase of play in great detail.[1]

CULTURAL GUIDELINES

The home is the cradle of cultural pursuits. The home climate can be a source of encouragement, it can be neutral, or it can create a wasteland. However, we cannot overlook the value of community agencies: recreation centers, settlement houses, art galleries, concert halls, and the schools. An innovative agency is Operation Headstart, which is of great value to disadvantaged children.

For the average child, we should seek a heightened appreciation of our culture. There should be no significant gap between the recreation leader and his charges. The importance of acknowledging the group's current cultural understandings and appreciations should not be forgotten; failure to do so can result in lost opportunities and even negative outcomes. We should seek a minimum amount of skill rather than marked proficiency. The satisfaction of being involved in a creative endeavor is probably more important than the degree of skill achieved, although skill can whet one's thirst for other, more advanced experiences.

Varied tastes and appreciations are desirable; they can be stimulated through graded and diversified experiences. The overriding objective is to elevate and enrich the cultural tastes of each individual.

Suggested Reading

AXLINE, VIRGINIA M., *Play Therapy.* Boston: Houghton Mifflin Company, 1947.

CORBIN, H. DAN, *Recreation Leadership,* 3rd ed. Englewood Cliffs, N.J.: Prentice-Hall, Inc., 1970.

HUIZINGA, JOHAN, *Homo Ludens: A Study of the Play Element in Culture.* Boston: Beacon Press, 1955.

KAPLAN, MAX, *Leisure in America: A Social Inquiry.* New York: John Wiley & Sons, Inc., 1960.

[1] Virginia M. Axline, *Play Therapy* (Boston: Houghton Mifflin Company, 1947), p. 16.

Lee, Robert, *Religion and Leisure in America.* Nashville, Tenn.: Abingdon Press, 1964.

Madow, Pauline, *Recreation in America.* New York: The H. W. Wilson Co., 1965.

Ottman, Robert W. *Music for Sight Singing.* Englewood Cliffs, N.J.: Prentice-Hall, Inc., 1965.

Pieper, Josef, *Leisure: The Basis of Culture.* New York: New American Library, 1964.

Rosenberg, Bernard, and D. M. White, *Mass Culture: The Popular Arts in America.* New York: The Free Press, 1957.

" IT'S NOW 8:45 A.M.....I'LL PICK YOU UP RIGHT
AFTER WORK AT 10:30 A.M....OKAY?"

chapter twelve

CHALLENGES
AND TRENDS

*Education has no more serious responsibility
than making adequate provision for
enjoyment of recreative leisure, not only for
the sake of the immediate health, but still
more if possible for the sake of its lasting
effect upon the habits of the mind.*

JOHN DEWEY

CHALLENGES

This book has described the present status of leisure and recreation in the United States. Our changing milieu affects our life styles, patterns of behavior, and leisure use. We know many facts about human behavior, but our knowledge is rarely incorporated into everyday leisure living. For instance, we know that mothers grow tired of being in the home, washing, cleaning, and cooking for their husbands and children seven days a week. Why not plan and organize recreation activities to help them through this situation? Recreation agencies have tried to enhance our lives through a variety of organized programs, but their effectiveness at improving the quality of life remains to be seen.

The biggest challenge is to improve our recreation programming. Present programs too often consist of activities designed to consume time, to fill idle hours with "busy" work, and to escape boredom, rather than positive, aggressive activity that would challenge people to change, to learn, and to develop. We need enlightened, bold leaders who plan and guide people's development rather than organize activities based entirely on popular demand.

We must put our accumulated knowledge to practical application while we experiment with programs, collect data, and report results. Great strides have been made in information storage and retrieval. The recreation leader is challenged to keep abreast of the flood of knowledge and add to it. The challenge of keeping all recreation employees up to date may be met by establishing a research and development department whose main concern is to keep employees informed and to circulate new findings. We need centralized information storage, available to local communities. Data should be collected on the effects of each activity on participants, evaluating people, programs, and facilities.

Can schedules be rearranged to allow the individual more latitude in his routine? Spreading the use of public facilities over a greater number of hours would decrease congestion, reducing frustrations and pressures that contribute to health problems. One change would be to open recreation centers twenty-four hours a day; the constant availability of attractive leisure might help change people's routines. We must examine our facilities to determine what changes in operation will affect the leisure lives of the most people.

Do we dare change our basis of pay from a time-centered one to some other form? Perhaps we could allow individual employees to set their time and schedule requirements by assigning them responsibility for a task but not dictating when or how they must accomplish it. Could the file clerk come to work at 4 PM, work until he had filed everything, and then go home? Suppose he came at 4 PM and finished by 8. Would he still be paid the normal amount? Would he be considered for promotion? Changes in schedule must be accompanied by a corresponding change in attitude toward work.

Are recreation employers responsible for encouraging their personnel to develop leisure pursuits for a higher quality of life? Presently when recreation leaders meet, their main topic of conversation is how hard they work. Long hours at small pay do not lead to an exciting life. A good start toward that goal has been made by designing facilities which attract individuals and require little supervision or organization. Additional facilities and materials must be designed to encourage people's participation in a variety of activities. Witness the increasing number of adult and family games, such as Cribbage, designed to solicit action and sharpen skills. Can we design a lobby or social hall that makes people want to socialize?

Another challenge is to make all recreation facilities suitable for use by handicapped persons. Foresight is needed in planning and design to make bathrooms, doorways, and furnishings sized to accommodate wheelchairs, stiff joints, poor eyesight, and so on. The handicapped 5 to 10 percent of our population usually have large amounts of leisure, but encounter problems in finding recreational outlets.

Another area of great challenge is the coordination of various community agencies. Groups which recognized a community need, offered and established a service, and now continue that service even though the need has changed should be reevaluated. We tend to be willing to add public services, but seldom to discontinue them.

Consider carefully the role of public recreation programs supported by local government, and how they should meet community needs. How much cooperation and coordination exists between public and private agencies? Many private agencies (Boy and Girl Scouts, YMCA, YWCA, Boys' Clubs, 4-H Clubs, churches, and so on) were formed around the turn of the century. Society has changed; its problems are different now. The Boy Scouts and Girl Scouts, the YMCA and the YWCA have continued as separate organizations. Should they combine to form coeducational programs? Have their services been taken over or offered on a broader scale by schools and governmental agencies?

The challenge of organizing or reorganizing leisure programs for communities is a function of local government. Local government must assure the citizens of a comprehensive leisure program for all, avoiding unnecessary duplication and affording equal opportunity for all.

Another challenge, particularly in large urban communities, is that of meeting the leisure needs of special groups. Unemployed, underemployed, and partially employed people have large amounts of free time, as do the elderly, the handicapped, and others.

The White House Conferences on Aging have consistently recognized the need for preparing people for semiretirement and retirement. Many retired people are at a loss as to how to use their increased leisure. Organized programs for retirement villages and nursing homes need great improvement; however, the greatest challenge is to make people recognize their needs before they reach retirement.

What is the place of private, commercial recreation? Some localities have private social clubs, athletic clubs, special interest clubs, political clubs, and so on for those who can afford to join them. We take pride in our private enterprise system. Is increased private enterprise the direction America should continue to pursue in leisure? Competition has been a characteristic of the past. Can cooperation gain greater recognition in our scale of values? There are many examples of government and private enterprise working together in the development and management of recreation areas. Leisure is such a vast field that all must cooperate to develop it.

The most important challenge of all is the job of educating people to accept and use leisure. Our programs and methods of presentation must reach all age groups, to change people's attitudes toward a higher value for leisure.

Can education for leisure be part of the curriculum in each of the school divisions—elementary, middle, senior high, junior college, university? The leisure unit should impress the student with the importance of leisure pursuits as developmental opportunities throughout life, and should concentrate on his immediate use of leisure so that it becomes an integral part of his daily living.

Our schools need to be year-around operations with increased continuing education opportunities for all age groups. We learn at all ages, and the idea of teaching for future use should be replaced with the pattern of continuing education for all throughout the year. Many people have begun to enroll in a new course every semester, just to keep learning.

Can we use local citizens (not teachers) to sponsor and conduct extracurricular clubs and organizations within the public schools, or should the schools return to teaching only practical skills and knowledge and leave participant club programs to other agencies in the community? For instance, varsity and intramural athletic programs have little practical connection with physical education programs. Athletic programs might operate better if they were organized under a community club or municipal recreation program. School drama programs could become affiliated with community theatre programs. Strong arguments support activities that involve a cross-sectional age group (community-wide) rather than a homogeneous age group (within the high school).

University courses that prepare leaders for leisure are desperately in need of revision. No longer can leisure be an adjunct to a traditional discipline (sociology, business, physical education, forestry, or the like); we must have recognized leisure specialists.

We must make use of the mass media to spread our ideas. Can you devise a leisure living program as effective as "Sesame Street," or a series of cassette tape programs of instruction in various skills and interests? The paperback book on leisure living that becomes a best-seller will have great educational impact.

Research, a vital part of education for leisure, needs to be developed further. However, with tax sources drying up, competition from other fields is becoming acute. It is the job of the researcher to discover how we can prepare individuals for the future. How can individuals become more resilient and adaptable, able to meet the strain of crowded living conditions? At present, 75 percent of the population of the United States, or about 150 million people, live in 10 percent of the land area; concentration will probably grow even more intense.

We are told that everything that exists can be measured. How can we measure and diagnose an individual's recreational needs and prepare an appropriate leisure-time program for him? The State of Indiana feeds into a computer the characteristics of patients in its mental institutions, and the computer lists suitable activities for each patient. However, institutions often emphasize therapy at the expense of enjoyment. When we consider that forms of recreation are as broad as human interests, we realize the difficulty of programming activities for healthy individuals.

There are several services that will, after examining a form filled out by a client, prescribe leisure-time pursuits according to his interests. Even in the age of computers, however, there will always be a need for professionals to interpret and personalize the recommendations of computers. Such professional prescriptions obviously call for meticulous diagnoses.

TRENDS

The shortened workday and work week along with longer vacations and sabbaticals have had a "bullish" effect on recreation. Energy-saving devices make us more efficient at work; advanced medical and surgical care mean that we will have more leisure time as a result of a longer life. The average educational level of the population has increased by approximately two grades during each generation. All these trends have positively influenced the leisure-recreation movement. Other factors are listed below.

1. Cities throughout the United States are experiencing urban blight and sprawl, disintegrating instead of growing.

2. There is growing use of schools as recreation centers for the entire community, involving all age groups.

3. There is mounting evidence of listlessness and boredom among large numbers of young people. The National Institute of Mental Health reports growing dissatisfaction with work, play, family and sex life.

4. Americans seek more active leisure pursuits. Droves of them walk the hiking trails or go jogging or bicycling, and there has been a phenomenal increase in interest in tennis. Enthusiasts of such active sports use the term *preventive cardiology.*

5. Fringe benefits are a major consideration in job bargaining. More pleasant working conditions, longer vacations, a shorter work week, sick leave, pensions, and industrial recreation are prominent employee requirements.

6. Planning to restore and prevent further destruction of our environment must receive greater emphasis. Increased population pressures and technological advancement must be regulated.

7. Cultural programs such as symphony orchestras and dance, opera, and theatrical groups are being subsidized increasingly not only by individual patrons and foundations but also by municipalities, states, and the federal government; aesthetic and cultural uplift are among the results.

8. Americans approach leisure-time pursuits frenetically. Evidence mounts of our overuse of gadgets and overscheduling of our off-the-job lives.

9. The increased mobility of our populace (each year one of every four families moves to a new home) shows the need for activities where friendships can be made while people are involved in satisfying experiences. Community recreation, more than any other agency, provides such activities.

10. More discretionary income and time are likely in the future; even now the four-day and even three-day work week are spreading. They may yield enriched living opportunities, or they may backfire. Affluence brings a tendency to select more costly pursuits, such as sailing, motor boating, skiing on snow and water, scuba diving, horseback riding, flying, photography, travel, and owning vacation homes.

11. Communitywide activities for the handicapped and emotionally and mentally ill are becoming more common.

12. Government agencies at the federal and state levels are bound to become increasingly involved in recreational planning and services; they will continue to supplement and complement the services of the municipal and county departments.

13. The attitude of the public toward leisure will continue to change. With the satisfactions of work gradually diminishing as our economy becomes more automated, we are placing greater significance in leisure-time

activities. Each individual must find the balance of activities suitable for him, including arts and sports. As leisure occupies a greater portion of our lives, we will become more selective, choosing pursuits that help us achieve serenity and contemplation.

14. Recreation planning will grow more international in scope. Conferences such as those held periodically by the International Federation of Park and Recreation Administration, the International Council of Health, Physical Education and Recreation, and the International Recreation Association reflect common concerns.

15. Additional recreational facilities are needed for several reasons: (1) more people participate in leisure activities; (2) each person has an expanding variety of interests; (3) leisure time is expanding; (4) there is a large assortment of pleasure vehicles at our disposal, such as skimobiles, motor homes, dune buggies, and campers; (5) special interests such as boating, skiing, and golf require large areas of water or land.

16. Education for leisure will become a subject area in school systems. The authors have sensed this need from the very inception of this project, and it has been their major goal in writing this book.

These are but a few of the challenges and trends confronting the professional recreation-leisure leader who earnestly wants to add to the quality of life through leisure living. There is so much to do—let's get on with it!

TEACHING MODULE
FOR
EDUCATION
FOR LEISURE

This module is designed for use with individualized instruction in a unit on leisure living in public high schools and community colleges, and in units on introduction to recreation careers in vocational-technical schools, community colleges, and for recreation and park department workers and employees of private agencies.

INTRODUCTION

No universally accepted format exists for teaching modules (also termed *contract teaching* or *individualized instruction*). This module organizes the material in this book in a logical sequence. Each specific objective in the module includes materials keyed to this text and to other references, suggested activities, and a method of evaluation to determine if the objective has been reached. Life styles vary greatly; this module leaves the teacher flexible enough to adapt to local situations.

RATIONALE

We live in a highly organized, complex society where physical pressures—crowded conditions, noise, pollution, disease, economic strain, traffic congestion, and so on—create psychological problems and mar the quality of life. Our basic personal demands—for food, rest, elimination, and so on—remain fairly constant. Technological advances have made it possible to reduce the work we must do, which increases our leisure.

Many people do not know what to do with their increased leisure. They need guidance in analyzing their situation to determine a course of action that will enhance their lives. They must know themselves before they can effectively help others. To achieve this end, understanding leisure and self, this module is designed.

MATERIALS

This module is based on *Education for Leisure* by Corbin and Tait. School libraries or materials centers should have copies of the bibliographical materials listed at the end of each chapter. Many local recreation departments have professional materials which can supply more detailed information on subjects summarized in the text. Each assignment suggestion included in the module objectives refers to a text chapter to indicate a main source of information and one supplemental resource of particular value.

UNIT OBJECTIVE

To know my basic needs and recognize the factors that motivate my choice of activities for leisure.

Specific objectives

1. To define and understand the terms

2. To determine the relative importance of leisure in my daily living pattern
3. To understand basic human development patterns and identify my present position in those patterns
4. To identify and inventory my leisure living skills and knowledge to determine how well prepared I am to participate in leisure living
5. To know my local community outlets for leisure
   a. To identify facilities for individual leisure pursuits, such as parks, museums, libraries, the home, and commercial facilities
   b. To know the purpose and extent of programs organized for group participation by schools, YMCA, scouts, church, city, clubs, and so on
6. To determine what changes I should make in my leisure living

PROCEDURES

1. Define and understand terms.

   a. Identify key words such as *leisure, free time, obligated time, recreation.*
   b. Compare textbook definitions with dictionary definitions.
   c. Gather the definitions and thoughts of people in your community: young and old, men and women, rich and poor, black and white, employed and unemployed, and so on.

Materials: CORBIN and TAIT, *Education for Leisure,* Chapter 1.
NASH, J. B., *Recreation: Pertinent Readings,* Chapters 1, 5.

Evaluation: Define *leisure, free time, play, obligated time, recreation.* Mark true or false:

1. Leisure is most available to rich people.
2. Adult working men have no need to play.
3. Selected recreation activities can help cure schizophrenia.
4. A public recreation program can sponsor only socially acceptable activities.
5. Unobligated time is the same as free time.
6. *Recreation* and *leisure* are synonymous.
7. People who follow routines soon grow bored.
8. The individual must be taught the skills for an activity before he will participate in that leisure activity.
9. The mechanization of industry has made a minor contribution toward expanding our leisure time.
10. An economic surplus creates more free time for a large segment of our society.

2. *Determine the relative importance of leisure in my daily living pattern.*

   a. Write a careful, honest statement of your personal views on the place of leisure in your life. Defend your statement to a diverse group of at least five other people.

   b. Keep a daily diary for at least a week, recording fifteen-minute intervals. (See Table 1.) Categorize your activities as: (1) personal existence (sleep, eat, bathe, groom, and so on); (2) subsistence (work, school, and so on); (3) leisure (relaxation, recreation, play, and so on). Analyze your results. Do they reflect the position you stated in *a*? Was this a typical week? If not, why not?

   c. Itemize your expenses during the week according to the categories in *b*. Are these costs compatible to statement *a*?

   d. Visit at least one: your local mental health clinic, counseling service, welfare office, church pastor, and jail. Answer the question, "Is leisure a problem to those who are experiencing personal difficulties?"

Materials: CORBIN and TAIT, *Education for Leisure,* Chapter 1.
               BRIGHTBILL, CHARLES K., *The Challenge of Leisure,* Chapter 2.

Evaluation: Rank the following phrases in their order of importance to you:

have enough money to buy anything I want (economic independence)
know how to do many things (education)
have many friends (popularity)
be physically fit and healthy (good health)
produce something that someone else needs (work)
believe that a supreme being will care for me (religion)
lead a balanced life (no extreme commitments)
enjoy life to its fullest (fun)

Write a brief essay on the importance of leisure to you.
How much time do you spend *daily* (during the week) on:

Sleep _____ hours = _____%
Eating _____ hours = _____%
Grooming _____ hours = _____%
Work-Study _____ hours = _____%
Recreation _____ hours = _____%
Transportation _____ hours = _____%

TABLE 1. "How my time flies." *Instructions:* Place in the boxes the total hours you spend each day in the various categories. Some activities may be difficult to classify, but be sure you account for a grand total of 24 hours each day. Few people can recall activities for more than three days; therefore, we suggest you use Monday and Friday mornings to record yours.

	Monday	Tuesday	Wednesday	Thursday	Friday	Saturday	Sunday	Average
Personal								
Sleep								
Eat								
Grooming (bathe, etc.)								
Subtotal								
Subsistence								
Work								
School- study								
Travel (to and from)								
Subtotal								
Leisure								
Obligated (organizations)								
Scheduled (travel, hobbies)								
Free time								
Other								
Subtotal								
Grand total								
Money spent during leisure								

If you had one hundred dollars and the next twenty-four hours free, what would you do?

3. *Understand basic human development patterns and identify my present position in those patterns.*

   a. Briefly explain Erikson's eight stages of development and assign a reasonable age range to each stage. Place someone you know in each stage.
   b. List outstanding events of your life, starting at the present and going backward to your birth. Give your age at the time of each event.
   c. Where do you fit into the development stages? Have three other people who know you well place you in the stage they think fits you best.
   d. Select an older person you know extremely well: father, mother, brother, sister, uncle, grandparent. Would you like to change his pattern of living? Why? What improvements do you think would enhance his life?

Materials: CORBIN and TAIT, *Education for Leisure,* Chapter 3.
               BISCHOF, LEDFORD J., *Adult Psychology,* Chapter 1.
Evaluation: List the characteristics of a 70-year-old female, a 40-year-old male, a 13-year-old girl, a 2½-year-old boy.

Suppose you were to organize basketball teams in your community. What leagues would you set up, and what criteria for players in each league would assure equal competition?

What leisure facilities would you recommend for an isolated armed service base housing 2,000 young single males? Which facilities would be most important?

4. *Identify and inventory my leisure living skills and knowledge to determine how well prepared I am to participate in leisure living.*

   a. Check your opinions and attitudes by taking self-tests, such as the one in Corbin, *Recreation Leadership,* p. 77.
   b. Evelute in writing your participant skills in the following fields:
      (1) *Music.* Can you sing, play an instrument, discuss the latest hits and performers?
      (2) *Art.* Can you mix colors, draw, photograph, carve, design?
      (3) *Dance.* Can you waltz, fox trot, watusi, rhumba, cha-cha, square-dance?
      (4) *Repair skills and crafts.* Can you fix a car, build a shelf, repair plumbing or a radio, tie-dye, sew, knit, cook?
      (5) *Sports.* Are you physically fit? Can you play tennis, golf, billiards, basketball, baseball? Skate, ski, swim, dive, tumble?

(6) *Nature.* Can you identify birds, flowers, stars, rocks, shells, animals, fish? Can you camp, shoot, row, sail, garden?

(7) *Games.* Can you play chess, checkers, bridge, poker, rummy, monopoly, table tennis, horseshoes?

(8) *Social skills.* Do you read, write, converse about religion, politics, international affairs, travel?

c. Reexamine the analysis of your daily diary. Are you happy with your leisure activities? Would you like to try something for which you lack prerequisite skills? Develop a plan to begin the new activity. Can you logically justify it by your knowledge of your needs at your present stage of development?

d. Develop a leisure budget for yourself and your family.

Materials: CORBIN and TAIT, *Education for Leisure,* Chapter 11.
CORBIN, *Recreation Leadership,* Chapter 7.

Evaluation: How did you spend your leisure time last week? How many hours did you spend participating in the following activities?

Social contacts	Arts and crafts
Travel	Music
Sports	Hobbies
Reading	Organizations
	Other activities

Of what organizations are you a member? What activities do you enjoy on your own?

What would you like to do during leisure, that you have no opportunity to do now? List a series of steps you might take to help you accomplish this goal.

Where do you think you will be five years from now? What might your leisure activities be at that time?

How much did you spend last week for recreation? What percentage of your total expenses is that amount?

5. *Know my local community outlets for leisure.*

a. List the organizations in your community which sponsor recreation programs (YMCA, scouts, church, city, clubs, schools, and so on).

b. List commercial outlets such as movies, clubs, bars, bowling lanes, skating, and dancing.

c. List public facilities within a fifty-mile radius of your home (federal, state, and city parks, beaches, forests, zoos, museums, libraries, and so on).

    d. Interview the manager of a commercial outlet or the director of an organization to determine the impact of that operation on the community. How many of these outlets have you used?

Materials: CORBIN and TAIT, *Education for Leisure,* Chapters 5 through 9.

           MEYER, BRIGHTBILL, and SESSOMS, *Community Recreation: A Guide to Its Organization,* Chapters 10 through 20.

Evaluation: List the places in your community where you could do the following: play bridge, chess, billiards; find a partner for handball, tennis, dancing; join a team for basketball or softball; go canoeing, sailing, fishing, hunting, camping; learn to knit, sew, cook, sculpture, do ceramics; share ideas on world events, latest books, politics.

Are additional facilities and/or programs needed in your community? How would you recommend that the needed facility or program for your community be organized?

6. *What changes should I make in my leisure living?*

    a. Summarize your present leisure living pattern, using the material you have prepared for the preceding objectives.

    b. Write about your personal ambitions, describing the life style you believe would be most satisfying to you.

    c. Compare your summary of what you do with your description of what you would like to do.

Materials: CORBIN and TAIT, *Education for Leisure,* Chapters 2 and 12.

Evaluation: What part of my living pattern can I change?

More detailed information, including films, cassettes, pamphlets, and additional evaluation materials, is available from Dr. William J. Tait, P. O. Box 3952, Tallahassee, Florida 32303.

appendix two

THE
TWELVE-MONTH
SCHOOL

The year-round school spreads the use of a school plant over the entire year. Although there are a variety of year-round plans, that of the Valley View School District in Romeoville, Illinois merits mention. The 45–15 plan developed in Romeoville appears to be suited to the variable midwestern weather. Under this plan, pupils are divided into four groups. Each group attends school for 45 days and then has a 15-day vacation. During each calendar year, each teacher and student is scheduled for four sessions totaling 180 days. The attendance timetables of the groups are staggered so that on any school day only three groups are in attendance. Classrooms and buses are scheduled and used on a year-round basis. Teachers are also given several contract and schedule options. By using the 45–15 plan, the Valley View District has saved itself the cost of constructing and equipping 76 new classrooms.

Four-quarter (or trimester) plans are more common in warm climates such as Georgia, Florida, and California, although a few colder-weather cities have adopted such plans (and conversely, some cities in warmer climates use 45–15 plans). The following list of school districts, although incomplete, reflects the swing toward the year-round school.

Chula Vista, California	45–15
LaMesa, California	45–15
Valley View, Illinois	45–15
Francis Howell, St. Charles, Missouri	45–15
Mora, Minnesota	45–15
Northville, Michigan	45–15
Prince William County, Virginia	45–15
Monassa, Georgia	45–15
Hinesburg, Vermont	45–15
Chicago, Illinois (four schools)	45–15
Jefferson County, Louisville, Kentucky	Four-quarter
Atlanta, Georgia	Four-quarter
Rochester, Pennsylvania	Four-quarter
Hayward, California	Four-quarter
Mollalla, Oregon	Four-quarter
Dade County, Florida	Trimester

The Atlanta, Georgia school system is another good example of the twelve-month school plan, also termed the *flexible school year*. Atlanta has had such a plan since September 1968. Pupils are required to attend school for three quarters during the year, and are encouraged to attend the fourth quarter also. Secondary schools have three twelve-week quarters and one ten-week summer session. Tuition is charged for summer-quarter attendance. The objectives of the Atlanta plan are flexibility and quality in education.

Educators have been the prime movers in the trend toward the twelve-month school plan. Its implications for park and recreation personnel as well as school personnel are staggering. For example, the flexible school year provides opportunity for intensive experiences in outdoor education, camping, nature lore, hiking, backpacking, and ecology study. The meaningful application of the so-called "academic subjects"—biology (botany and zoology), geology, and astronomy (involving mathematics as well as art and photography)—reveals the close relationship between recreation and education.

Expanding the school year will probably result in greater school use of parks and recreation facilities, in addition to greater reciprocal use of school facilities by recreation departments. Such overlapping community use of publicly-owned facilities is long overdue. We can hardly justify using tax-supported facilities for only a portion of the day, week, and year.

A 1972 Gallup poll of public attitudes toward education showed that a majority of parents favor keeping schools open the year around.[1] Parental opposition often vanished when parents discovered that the new plan would not interfere with family vacations. The Gallup question was worded as follows: "To utilize school buildings to the full extent, would you favor keeping the school open the year around? Each student would attend school for nine months over the course of a year. Do you approve or disapprove?" The nationwide results showed that 53 percent of parents approved, 41 percent disapproved, and 6 percent had no opinion. Professional educators were even more favorably inclined toward the proposal: 66 percent approved, 30 percent disapproved, and 4 percent had no opinion. That the trend is toward the year-around concept is revealed by comparing the preceding figures with those of a 1970 poll, which showed only 42 percent of the nation's adults in favor of the twelve-month school, 52 percent not in favor, and 4 percent with no opinion.

The 1972 Gallup poll also posed the following question: "In most communities students can learn many things outside the school. Would you approve or disapprove if the schools here reduced the amount of classroom instruction to allow students to make greater use of the educational opportunities outside the school?" Of the parents polled, 56 percent approved, 35 percent disapproved, and 9 percent had no opinion. However, 72 percent of the professional educators approved, only 26 percent disapproved, and 2 percent had no opinion.

The twelve-month school plan will certainly be a catalyst for more productive use of school and recreational facilities in the future.

[1] *Phi Delta Kappan,* LIV, No. 1 (September 1972), 33–46.

SUGGESTED
MINIMAL RESOURCES
IN EDUCATION
FOR LEISURE
FOR A HIGH
SCHOOL LIBRARY

PHILOSOPHY

BRANTLEY, H., and H. DOUGLAS SESSOMS, *Recreation, Issues and Perspectives.* Columbia, S.C.: Wing Publications, 1969.

BRIGHTBILL, CHARLES K., *The Challenge of Leisure.* Englewood Cliffs, N.J.: Prentice-Hall, Inc., 1963.

KRAUS, RICHARD, *Recreation and Leisure in Modern Society.* New York: Appleton-Century Crofts, 1971.

LARRABEE, ERIC, and ROLF MEYERSOHN, eds., *Mass Leisure.* New York: The Free Press, 1958.

NASH, JAY B., *The Philosophy of Recreation and Leisure.* Dubuque, Iowa: William C. Brown Company, Publishers, 1960.

ADMINISTRATION

ATHLETIC INSTITUTE, *Planning Facilities for Health, Physical Education and Recreation.* Chicago: Athletic Institute, 1965.

173

BANNON, JOSEPH J., *Problem Solving in Recreation and Parks.* Englewood Cliffs, N.J.: Prentice-Hall, Inc., 1973.

HJELTE, GEORGE, and JAY S. SHIVERS, *Public Administration of Park and Recreation Services.* New York: The Macmillan Company, 1963.

NATIONAL RECREATION AND PARK ASSOCIATION, *Management Aid Series* (96 manuals). Arlington, Va.: National Recreation and Park Association.

VAN DER SMISSEN, BETTY, *Legal Liability of Cities and Schools for Injuries in Recreation and Parks.* Cincinnati: The W. H. Anderson Co., 1968.

PROGRAM AND LEADERSHIP

ATHLETIC INSTITUTE, *The Recreation Program,* 2nd ed. Chicago: Athletic Institute, 1965.

CORBIN, H. DAN, *Recreation Leadership,* 3rd ed. Englewood Cliffs, N.J.: Prentice-Hall, Inc., 1970.

CRATTY, BRYANT J., and JAMES E. BREEN, *Educational Games for Handicapped Children.* Denver: Love Publishing Co., 1972.

DANFORD, HOWARD, and MAX SHIRLEY, *Creative Leadership in Recreation,* 2nd ed. Boston: Allyn & Bacon, Inc., 1970.

MEYER, HAROLD D., CHARLES K. BRIGHTBILL, and H. DOUGLAS SESSOMS, *Community Recreation: A Guide to Its Organization,* 4th ed. Englewood Cliffs, N.J.: Prentice-Hall, Inc., 1969.

MITCHELL, VIOLA, et al., *Camp Counseling,* 4th ed. Philadelphia: W. B. Saunders Company, 1970.

PERIODICALS

For periodicals appropriate for both high school and college libraries, see Suggested Minimal Resources in Education for Leisure for a College Library.

SUGGESTED
MINIMAL RESOURCES
IN EDUCATION
FOR LEISURE
FOR A COLLEGE
LIBRARY

AMERICAN ASSOCIATION OF HEALTH, PHYSICAL EDUCATION AND RECREATION, *Leisure and the Quality of Life.* Washington, D.C.: AAHPER, 1972.

BANNON, JOSEPH J., *Problem Solving in Recreation and Parks.* Englewood Cliffs, N.J.: Prentice-Hall, Inc., 1973.

BEACH, DALE S., *Personnel: The Management of People at Work.* New York: The Macmillan Company, 1965.

BRIGHTBILL, CHARLES K., *Man and Leisure.* Englewood Cliffs, N.J.: Prentice-Hall, Inc., 1961.

CARNEGIE COMMISION ON HIGHER EDUCATION, *Less Time, More Options.* New York: McGraw-Hill Book Company, 1971.

CASE, MAURICE, *Recreation for Blind Adults.* Springfield, Ill.: Charles C Thomas, Publisher, 1966.

CHAPMAN, FRED, *Recreation for the Handicapped.* New York: The Ronald Press Company, 1960.

CLAWSON, MARION, and JACK KNETSCH, *Economics of Outdoor Recreation.* Baltimore: The Johns Hopkins Press, 1966.

CORBIN, H. DAN, *Recreation Leadership,* 3rd ed. Englewood Cliffs, N.J.: Prentice-Hall, Inc., 1970.

DeGrazia, Sebastian, *Of Time, Work and Leisure.* New York: The Twentieth Century Fund, 1962.

Doell, Charles E., *Elements of Park and Recreation Administration.* Minneapolis, Minn.: Burgess Publishing Co., 1963.

Dubin, R., et al., *Leadership and Productivity.* San Francisco: Chandler Publishing Co., 1965.

Faught, Millard C., *More Timewealth for You.* New York: Pyramid Publications, 1969.

Fromm, Eric, *May Man Prevail.* Garden City, N.Y.: Doubleday & Company, Inc., 1964.

Gabrielsen, M. Alexander, ed., *Swimming Pools: A Guide to Their Planning, Design and Operation.* Ft. Lauderdale, Fla.: Hoffman Publications, Inc., 1969.

Gabrielsen, M. Alexander, and Caswell M. Miles, *Sports and Recreation Facilities.* Englewood Cliffs, N.J.: Prentice-Hall, Inc., 1958.

Gabrielsen, M. Alexander, Betty Spears, and B. W. Gabrielsen, *Aquatics Handbook,* 2nd ed. Englewood Cliffs, N.J.: Prentice-Hall, Inc., 1968.

Galbraith, John K., *The New Industrial State.* Boston: Houghton Mifflin Company, 1967.

Gibson, W. H., *Recreational Programs for Summer Camps.*

Haun, Paul, *Recreation: A Medical Viewpoint.* New York: Teachers College, Columbia University Press, 1965.

Hjelte, George, and Jay S. Shivers, *Public Administration of Park and Recreation Services.* New York: The Macmillan Company, 1963.

Hoffer, Eric, *The Temper of Our Time.* New York: Harper & Row, Publishers, 1967.

Kaplan, Max, *Leisure in America.* New York: John Wiley and Sons, Inc., 1960.

Kleindienst, Viola K., and Arthur Weston, *Intramural and Recreation Programs for Schools and Colleges.* New York: Appleton-Century-Crofts, 1964.

Kraus, Richard G., *Recreation and the Schools.* New York: The Macmillan Company, 1964.

———, *Recreation Today: Program Planning and Leadership.* New York: Appleton-Century-Crofts, 1966.

Maslow, Abraham, *Toward a Psychology of Being.* New York: Van Nostrand Reinhold Company, 1968.

Mead, Margaret, *Culture and Commitment.* Garden City, N.Y.: Doubleday & Company, Inc., 1970.

Meyer, Harold D., and Charles K. Brightbill, *Recreation Administration: A Guide to Its Practices.* Englewood Cliffs, N.J.: Prentice-Hall, Inc., 1956.

Meyer, Harold D., Charles K. Brightbill, and H. Douglas Sessoms, *Community Recreation: A Guide to Its Organization,* 4th ed. Englewood Cliffs, N.J.: Prentice-Hall, Inc., 1969.

MILLER, NORMAN P., and DUANE M. ROBINSON, *The Leisure Age.* Belmont, Calif.: Wadsworth Publishing Co., Inc., 1963.

NASH, JAY B., *Philosophy of Recreation and Leisure.* Dubuque, Iowa: William C. Brown Company, Publishers, 1960.

———, *Recreation: Pertinent Readings.* Dubuque, Iowa: William C. Brown Company, Publishers, 1965.

Outdoor Recreation for America, Report to the President and Congress by the Outdoor Recreation Resources Review Commission, Vols. I and XXII. Washington, D.C.: U.S. Government Printing Office, 1962.

POMEROY, JANET, *Recreation for the Physically Handicapped.* New York: The Macmillan Company, 1964.

POOR, RIVA, *Four Days, Forty Hours.* Cambridge, Mass.: Bursk and Poor, 1970.

RIESMAN, DAVID, *Abundance for What.* Garden City, N.Y.: Doubleday & Company, Inc., 1964.

RODNEY, LYNN S., *Administration of Public Recreation.* New York: The Ronald Press Company, 1964.

SHIVERS, JAY S., *Camping.* New York: Appleton-Century-Crofts, 1971.

———, *Principles and Practices of Recreational Service.* New York: The Macmillan Company, 1967.

TOYNBEE, ARNOLD, *Change and Habit: The Challenge of Our Time.* New York: Oxford University Press, 1966.

THE TWENTIETH CENTURY FUND, *New Towns: Laboratories for Democracy.* New York: The Twentieth Century Fund, 1971.

VAN DER SMISSEN, BETTY, *Legal Liability of City and Schools for Injuries in Recreation and Parks.* Cincinnati, Ohio: The W. H. Anderson Co., 1968.

VANNIER, MARYHELEN, *Methods and Materials in Recreation Leadership.* Belmont, Calif.: Wadsworth Publishing Co., Inc., 1966.

WHYTE, WILLIAM H., Jr., *The Organization Man.* Garden City, N.Y.: Doubleday & Company, Inc., 1957.

YUKIC, THOMAS, *Fundamentals of Recreation.* New York: Harper & Row, Publishers, 1963.

PERIODICALS FOR HIGH SCHOOL AND COLLEGE

Behavior Today, P.O. Box 2993, Boulder, Colo. 80302.

Journal of Health, Physical Education and Recreation, American Association of Health, Physical Education and Recreation, 1201 Sixteenth Street, N.W., Washington, D.C. 20036.

Journal of Leisure Research, National Recreation and Parks Association, 1601 N. Kent Street, Arlington, Va. 22209.

Parks and Recreation, National Recreation and Parks Association, 1601 N. Kent Street, Arlington, Va. 22209.

Psychology Today, CRM Books, P.O. Box 2990, Boulder, Colo. 80302.

Therapeutic Recreation Journal, National Recreation and Parks Association, 1601 N. Kent Street, Arlington, Va. 22209.

INDEX